Transitions
in the Lives of Jesuits
and Former Jesuits

Transitions
in the Lives of Jesuits and Former Jesuits

Collected and Edited by
Donald J. Foran

West Coast Compañeros, Inc.

Copyright © 2014 West Coast Compañeros, Inc.

The individual authors hold the copyright to their stories and poems.

All rights reserved. No part of this publication may be reproduced, stored in or introduced into a retrieval system, or transmitted in any form or by any means (electronic, mechanical, by photocopying, recording or otherwise) without the prior written permission of the author.

ISBN-10: 1-4947-9106-4
ISBN-13: 978-1-4947-9106-3

Questions or comments can be directed to westcoastcompaneros@gmail.com

http://westcoastcompanions.org

The cover image, the painting "Morning Peace," is used courtesy of the artist, Debra Van Tuinen. http://www.vantuinenart.com

An excerpt from *The Nonviolent Life* by John Dear is used by kind permission of Pace e Bene Press: http://paceebene.org/shop/the-nonviolent-life

The Bob Holstein quotes in the Preface are drawn from Brigid Barry's article "Companions" in the Fall 2000 issue of *Company* magazine

We wish to dedicate this book to all the Jesuits, current and former, who have been our Companions on the journey. We remember especially Bob and Loretta Holstein and John Baumann, SJ, who were there with us in the beginning. They are now and ever will be in our hearts. We also honor Dan Berrigan, SJ, Bill Bichsel, SJ, Greg Boyle, SJ, Bob Brophy, Morgan Zo Callahan, Bill Wood, SJ, and all who have been inspired—and have inspired us to try—to live a faith that does justice.

Benediction

When I was in London decades ago, a crazy old man approached
As a friend and I sat talking near Westminster Cathedral.
He was wild-eyed, noisy, gesticulating, unkempt.
His flowing hair and beard gave him the appearance of an
Ancient prophet, slightly berserk, but clearly meaning no harm.
He was, I believed, quite drunk while we, with devastating sobriety,
Watched, a bit amused, as people scattered for shelter from his gaze.
As he rambled closer, I could distinguish his words, a Latin prayer,
"In nominee patris et filii . . ." and I saw his arm fly up
To shape in the misty London air a formal sign.
Some of those sitting by us told him to go away; others hoped
To pass the time by baiting him, urging on the mania and the man.
My friend observed, in lowered voice, how terribly drunk
The local vagrants can become. I said, "It's a blessing he's giving,"
And to the man, "Thank you." He pointed at me, made my blood freeze,
And shouted with undiluted passion, "He understands!"
And so, out of the welter of images, the wash of literary terms,
The torment of unresolved theological questions, self-doubt, love,
Illusion, I salvaged and pass on a mad-eyed benediction, hoping,
As that man did, that my hopes for you will be somehow understood.

                                                       Don Foran

Contents

Dedication	v
Benediction Don Foran	vii
Preface Robert R. Rahl	xv
Acknowledgments	xxi
Introduction L. Patrick Carroll	1
Hallowing Our Diminishments Thomas E. Ambrogi	5
A Night Dream Clarifies a Life's Dream Wilkie Au	9
Transition to Transformation John A. Baumann, SJ	13
Spiritual Change in Personal History Eugene C. Bianchi	17
From the Ground Up William J. Bichsel, SJ	21
Broadcasting, Religious Life, & Unpredictable Graces James A. Brown	25
An Unexpected Patriarch Edward L. Burke	31
One Life Morgan Zo Callahan	35
My Many Lives L. Patrick Carroll	39
Deciding Times Gary Chamberlain	43

Contents

A Jesuit Journey
John F. Christensen — 47

One Door Closed and Another Opened
Juanita Cordero — 51

Choosing to Live a Nonviolent Life
John S. Dear — 53

From Jesuit to Married Catholic Worker
Eric C. DeBode — 55

A Jesuit Falls in Love
John F. Devine — 59

Four Happy Turning Points
Joseph J. Feeney, SJ — 63

My 50th Anniversary as a Jesuit Priest
Paul Fitterer, SJ — 67

The Tree of Life is Green
Donald J. Foran — 71

Vocation Discernment
John Fuchs, SJ — 75

The First Night
James T. Gilroy — 79

Movement to New Possibilities
Peter J. Henriot, SJ — 81

Passing Brothers
Rodney P. Herold — 85

Celebrating 52 Years As a Jesuit
Patrick J. Howell, SJ — 89

Letter from McLeodganj, Himachal Pradesh
Kenneth Ireland — 93

Losing Faith
Michael R. Johnson — 97

Falling in Love
Robert Blair Kaiser — 101

Contents

Gratitude E. Paul Kelly	105
The Link That Binds All Together Michael E. Kennedy, SJ	109
David the "Matchmater" John B. Leira	111
The Look of Mary Robillard Raymond J. Leonardini	115
The Primacy of Intuition John LeSarge	117
Roads Taken John B. Lounibos	121
A.M.D.G. Kathleen M. MacPherson	123
A Grief Delayed G. Donald Maloney	127
Bus 68 John McConville	133
Much More the Jesuit Douglass D. McFerran	137
A Mudala in Zambia James P. McGloin, SJ	139
Mystery Ends Michael G. Merriman	145
The Primacy of Desire Joseph J. Mitchell	149
Nothing to Contribute Donald R. Moses	153
The CUA DMin Game Changer John P. Mossi, SJ	155
Stumbling on My Journey Dennis K. Mulvihill	157

Contents

Lynn George Muth, RIP July 17, 2011
Lynn & Heidi Muth 159

The Eighth Sacrament
Richard C. Pfaff 163

Not a Tame Lion
Robert R. Rahl 169

A New Language
James W. Riley 173

As Time Moves On
Antonio Salcido 175

Jiao
Michael R. Saso 179

Chips and Slivers
F. Joseph Schneider 183

Shedding Skin
Gary R. Schouborg 185

The Night That Changed My Life
Raymond A. Schroth, SJ 189

All Is Well
George Seeber 193

The Phantom of Seattle
Jerome B. Seitz 195

Chopsticks in Hand
Robert K. Semans 199

Fall Experiment: Moving Towards Vows
Lucas Sharma, nSJ 203

Steppingstones of Life
Carl J. Slawski 205

Late Night Thoughts on Leaving JRS
Gary N. Smith, SJ 209

"The Child in My Womb Leapt for Joy."
J. Michael Sparough, SJ 215

Contents

"B" Students Also Admitted
James R. Stickney — 219

The Problem
John F. Suggs — 223

Segue
William M. Sullivan — 233

Through the Ordinary
Patrick J. Twohy, SJ — 235

Then There Is Family
Mary Ann & Dave Van Etten — 237

Personal Statement
David W. Van Etten — 239

The Thing Itself
Nicholas J. Weber — 245

A Moment of Truth
Robert J. Willis — 249

The Common Good
William J. Wood, SJ — 253

Preface

Robert Mills Holstein Jr. was in the California Province for seven short years (1960–67), but Ignatian spirituality and the Jesuit orientation to a life of service for others made a deep and lasting imprint on his life. Bob was a man on fire with practical concern for others, and he always had a number of irons in the fire. One of his many projects became known as the Companions. Soon after leaving the Society, Bob became the focal point for a group of men, mostly former Jesuits but some still in the Society, who came primarily from the California and Oregon Provinces. They gathered periodically to enjoy each other's company, and to commiserate and support each other, offering healing to one other in their struggles to adapt to life after the Society—moving on in their lives as companions on a shared journey. The stories in this book distill meaningful moments in some of those journeys. The first meetings of the Companions were, in a way, therapy sessions for those who hadn't reconciled the feelings they had when they left. For some it was their first opportunity to express anger and disappointment towards the Jesuits. Others came to the meetings open and positive about their reasons for leaving and the choices they made. In a 2000 interview with *Company* magazine, Bob recalled those early days.

"In those first gatherings, everyone just talked, feeling their way. Everyone has a different, deeply personal reason for leaving. I left because I fell in love. Some guys leave because they can't handle the formation process, others because they can't live in community, others because they find that their vocation leads them to life outside the Jesuits. A lot of guys have no ax to grind; for others, it takes years to go through the process of healing. But they get over their negative feelings. They see we're just as Jesuit as we ever were—after all, we're all an accumulation of our own spiritual journeys."

Due to Bob's positive influence, the group's energy was not all directed inward, but spread out to embrace a number of good works and social-justice ministries. Over the course of two decades, there was a growing presence of the Companions and their families at the annual protests for the closure of the School of the Americas at Fort Benning, Georgia. Bob was instrumental in organizing the Ignatian Family Teach-Ins, held under a big tent during those protests. The Teach-Ins grew to include participants from all the Jesuit colleges and universities in the United States, along with students and teachers from a large number of Jesuit high schools and prep schools from across the country. In recent years, the Ignatian Solidarity Network has assumed responsibility for hosting the annual Ignatian Family Teach-In for Justice, now held in Washington, DC.

In 1997, Bob and his wife Loretta traveled to Italy with their children. Their itinerary included all the usual tourist places, with the addition of a visit to the Jesuit Curia in Rome to meet Jesuit superior general Fr. Peter-Hans Kolvenbach. Bob had been corresponding with Fr. Kolvenbach regularly, keeping him up-to-date on the activities of the Companions. In that *Company* magazine interview, Bob told the following story.

"I e-mailed Fr. Kolvenbach, telling him I was going to be in Rome, and he invited me to come see him. We had a great visit. I told him I was coming to share with him some of the ideas our guys have, and how we're getting involved in different work. I mentioned to him that many of the guys feel like they're as much a Jesuit as they ever were when they were in the Society. Fr. Kolvenbach told me, 'I think they are Jesuits. You don't leave; I really believe that. Ignatius recognized that laymen are at the core of the Society. Although it's not necessarily true canonically, I would say that they are Jesuits.'"

Many, but not all, Compañeros would make the same identification. In the same interview, Bob pointed out that the group defies easy pigeonholing.

"One characteristic of this brotherhood is its wild and fiercely maintained diversity. They are old and young, working and retired, gay and straight, married and divorced, with and without children, recovering alcoholics and drug addicts. They are lawyers and doctors, Episcopal priests, high school teachers, professors, psychiatrists, psychologists, underground Catholics and above-ground ones, Buddhists, writers and gardeners, contractors and tradesmen, developers, real estate brokers, and day-care providers."

To Holstein, the connection between all of these different lives was simple.

"We're just as Ignatian as ever, spiritually. We're formed by the *Exercises*, by the accumulation of our spiritual journeys. I feel the presence of God wherever I've been. Everything I've ever done has been informed by the way the Jesuits look at life. Anything you do is capable of bringing God into the world. That's how I live my life, and that's what stays with me."

In 1998, again spearheaded by Holstein, and based on his desire for the group to do more, the Companions were incorporated in the state of California as a 501(c)(3) not-for-profit charitable organization: West Coast Compañeros, Inc. (WCCI), better known as the Companions or the Compañeros. The Companions, a network of former Jesuits (along with a few current Jesuits) initially from the ten western states, has grown to number close to eight hundred members. Thanks to the Internet, that number now includes men (and women) from all over North, Central, and South America, as well as Europe, Africa, and Asia. A lively online discussion group ties the participants together from day to day, with the topics ranging from current

Preface

events to church renewal and reform, social justice, spirituality, poetry, and the challenges of aging. Because spouses and partners are welcome at the annual reunion-for-renewal, the "Compañeras" have also become valued members of the family.

The mission of this organization can be summarized by one of our primary objectives, as formulated by Bob Holstein in the articles of incorporation: "To seek opportunities to establish programs in conjunction with the Society of Jesus and other groups affiliated with its vision and commitment to alleviate poverty, to educate, to promote human and civil rights, and to achieve social justice." Bob saw the Companions as a group that, at times, would work hand in hand with the Jesuits, but independent and free to move on its own, united with the Society by a common Ignatian spirit: a faith that does justice. Beginning with Tom Smolich, SJ, recent California provincials have recognized the partnership opportunity that the Compañeros offer. They have encouraged closer connections between the province and WCCI by inviting us to send representatives to province convocations and social-ministry gatherings, and they have attended the Companions' annual meetings.

Bob Holstein lived long enough to see this organization get off the ground, but he died suddenly and without any warning in 2003, leaving a big hole in the hearts of all who knew him. In the eleven years since then, we have tried to keep his vision and spirit alive, especially in the annual get-togethers, and by supporting a number of social-justice works, some that were dear to Bob's heart, and others that have grown out of the same Ignatian spirit that inspired him. Some of these programs provide educational opportunities for street kids in Mexico, and poor young people in Guatemala and Honduras. One of the projects aims at supporting the indigenous survivors of the 1998 massacre in the Tzotzil village of Acteal in Chiapas,

Mexico. Another provides books, furnishings, and equipment for a school library in rural Kenya. You can see a complete list of those projects on our website at http://westcoastcompanions.org/projects.htm.

Jim Latham, SJ, was one of several current Jesuits who have formed a continuing connection with the Compañeros. From his longtime post in Paris, he listened in and occasionally participated in our online discussions. During one of his last visits to his home province, he joined the WCCI delegation to the 2003 California Province Convocation at Loyola Marymount University, and it was a delight to interact with him face to face. He also joined us at our Companions 2004 reunion. Jim died in 2009, just ten days after his eightieth birthday. About a year later, we received—completely out of the blue—an extraordinary gift of $17,000 from Jim's family, who were aware of his affection for this group. With no strings attached to the gift, we decided to form a small committee to develop simple guidelines and procedures for establishing a continuing grant program to provide modest support for some of our existing projects, and to encourage new grass-roots activities.

The Latham family's original gift was distributed over the course of four years, so we are doing ongoing fund-raising to ensure our ability to fund both new and continuing projects. If you wish to help, your tax-deductible donations, with checks made payable to WCCI Grant Program, can be sent to WCCI c/o Dave Van Etten, 702 Cree Drive, San Jose, CA 95123. All proceeds from the sale of this book, *Transitions in the Lives of Jesuits and Former Jesuits*, will go to support the activities of the grant program. Those who serve in these social-justice works, and those who benefit from their service, are grateful for your help and support.

Robert R. Rahl
California Province 1963–73
President, West Coast Compañeros, Inc.

Acknowledgments

The editor wants to thank Robert Rahl for all his encouragement, his extraordinary copy-editing and formatting skills, and his fine Preface. I also am grateful to L. Pat Carroll for his Introduction, to Jeremy Rahl for his cover design, to Debra van Tuinen for sharing her painting "Morning Peace" for use as the front cover image, and to Morgan Zo Callahan for providing "a third pair of eyes" on the text. Douglass McFerran and Eugene Bianchi deserve credit for providing the initial impetus for this project. Finally, I applaud my wife Maggie and all of our contributors, especially Mary Ann and Dave Van Etten, for their patience, goodness, and collaborative spirit.

Don Foran
July 31, 2014
Feast of St. Ignatius of Loyola

Introduction

L. Patrick Carroll

Some motives were quite simple; they wanted to be good, to serve, to make the world better, to save their own souls and those of others. Other motives were more complicated. From the catechetic tendencies of the time too many were riddled with guilt, or fear. Some were pressured by family expectations for a first-born or favored son, since to be a priest was a blessing on an entire extended family. Others entered with acknowledged or, in many cases, unacknowledged homosexual tendencies alien to their family faith, making an all-male community a potentially safe-haven.

In most of these young men the motives were unique amalgams of these and more. . . . Only much later, if ever, do any of us truly know why we do what we do. Writing the offerings for this book helped many discover and claim their initial impulses as well as their later real-life adjustments.

Lamentably, motives were rarely discussed with anyone else by those newly-arrived at the novitiate, the initial stage of Jesuit formation. Young men became interchangeable parts of "a long black line," experiencing the same outward reality: wearing long black dresses, called cassocks, talking in Latin, keeping silence, praying often, cut off from family and friends and women and "the world." Internal realities differed deeply, but unspoken then, they surfaced only later with mixtures of pain, confusion, relief and freedom.

Jesuit formation went on for from ten to thirteen or more years, loosening in each stage; some novices and scholastics left along the way. Others were eventually ordained, entered into ministry as teachers, pastors, missionaries, community-

Introduction

organizers, administrators. After Vatican II ended in the mid-sixties, almost everything changed: all their relationships—with themselves, with each other, with women, with the world around them. How each reacted to such dramatic transformation differed, again, from man to man, but all were profoundly impacted. This book honors the struggles and successes of Jesuits and former Jesuits not by assuming that they were wonderfully alike, but that they were wonderfully diverse despite their similar training. Some of these men, now in their 90s, 80s, 70s, 60s, and 50s, a few younger still, found their vowed lives fulfilling and rewarding, and celebrate milestones much as married couples celebrate anniversaries. Their loved ones and the communities they have lived in celebrate along with them, and for good reason.

Some grasped desperately to maintain what they had come to cherish with the security that afforded, trying, often unsuccessfully, to keep the new evolving, sometimes intimidating, church and world at bay. Others embraced the myriad changes, letting go of whatever previous identity the past had afforded. Most danced between these extremes—but, again, none were left untouched. In 1975 and beyond, the Jesuits were quite different from what they had been in 1945, or '50 or '55 or '60. The church was different. For one thing, about 60% of the men they knew in formation had left. The priest's role was quite transformed. Relationships between men and women were more open and more complicated. The long black line no longer existed. Most men now were individual, isolated questers for real community, real companionship, honest intimacy whether within or outside that Society of Jesus.

Most carried with them scars from the past, but also values, gifts, hopes, and a deep sense of continued community with those with whom they had shared their Jesuit past. The vision usually remained even if in new forms—the undying hope of becoming "men for others," the search for "the *Magis*" i.e., the more, in whatever work or ministry they undertook, the desire to discover God (or some spark of the transcendent good) wherever they were and whatever they did. Most held onto a desire to be part of building a better world, building, in Ignatian language, a Kingdom. Most remained spiritual in orientation, though frequently finding their base outside familiar Catholic or even Christian structures.

These are their attempts to "capture" the key moments, inside or outside the Society, which made them who they are today. Their stories capture in myriad ways what was happening in the church and in the wider world in the latter part of the twentieth century and into the twenty-first. Each story, unique in itself, has universal ramifications not merely for these men, but, hopefully, for everyone who lived through or wants to understand a critical epoch of the Catholic Church and the world it inhabits.

Reading these stories of transitions in the lives of a particular, quite specific group of human beings can shed light on what it means for anyone to be human—changing, growing, searching.

In or out of the Catholic Church, in or out of the Society of Jesus, married or single, straight or gay, still vibrant and working, or aging and frail, all have come to know, each in a unique, yet harmonious way, the truth of poet Robert Frost's words in "Birches":

Earth's the right place for love:
I don't know where it's likely to go better.

Hallowing Our Diminishments

Thomas E. Ambrogi

Now in my 84th year, I reflect often on aging and the journey into our wholeness—on the elder years that are unique to each of us, these years of our seasoning, in the fantastic growth cycle that was gifted to each of us in the moment of our creation.

Years ago, when I was still a promising young man and not particularly concerned about growing old, I remember being deeply moved by Teilhard de Chardin's prayerful reflections on growing old in *The Divine Milieu*.

To be aware of the unity of all things in Christ, Teilhard says, is to be aware that, in the first half of our lives, we must "divinize our activities," become one with the redeeming Christ in all that we do. In the second half of our lives, our call is to "hallow our diminishments," learn to sanctify our "passivities." This is really a remarkable and exciting vision, worth meditating on in our elder years.

Hallowing is a wonderful word. It means "to make holy, to consecrate." A secondary meaning is: "to respect greatly, to venerate."

Diminishments refer to all those things that gradually fade from our grasp as we grow older. Teilhard mentions four: 1) the loss of persons dear to us; 2) the loss of our traditional persona, of the identity that has made us who we are before others; 3) the gradual dimming or loss of our physical and mental powers—and, finally, 4) the ultimate diminishment, which is death.

First, the experience of bereavement, of grieving. The pain of grieving for the death, or the going away, of a person who has been dear to me, one with whom my life has been deeply intertwined: the

Hallowing Our Diminishments

loss of a spouse, a parent, a child, a lover, a soul-mate friend.

To hallow the diminishment I feel at the loss of one most dear first demands a "letting go," as painfully difficult as that is. It is to commit myself to the work of grieving, letting myself feel deeply the loss in the fabric of my being, how I am bereft, made infinitely the poorer by the loss of that dear person's presence within me.

But hallowing that diminishment, making it holy, respecting it greatly, consecrating it, means to break through to embracing and welcoming something found—or, rather, something given by the grace of God. And that something given and unexpectedly found comes with immersing myself and all of my terrible pain in the breadth and length and height and depth and love which is the reality of being "filled with all the fullness of God," as Paul said to the Ephesians.

For elders, this bereavement often comes in the loss of status I experience as I am forced to put down all the trappings of my work, my career, my profession. I experience it as a loss of my own persona. Nobody remembers who I once was. I am no longer a _____. I remember, when I resigned my formal priestly ministry many years ago, that I was profoundly moved by no longer being "Father Tom." I now just try to be a priestly person, and that will have to do.

But perhaps the most difficult of diminishments is the gradual weakening, and even loss, of one's physical and mental powers that so often comes with age.

For Teilhard, the key to learning to hallow my progressive physical and mental diminishments lies in a deeply spiritual level of acceptance—a positive claiming of them, even honoring them as my own. It is only then that something creative can be made of them: to treat the diminishment as a companion, so that I can afford a certain detachment toward it, with even a kind of playfulness.

In all of these diminishments, we gradually learn that we have to very explicitly "let go." I have to perform a formal and deeply personal ritual of saying "goodbye" in each case before I can say "hello," before I can complete the cycle of hallowing my diminishments.

The greatest of our challenges is the persistent call to recognize the individuality and the beauty of each one around us. I call for people to recognize me for who I am, for all that I have been in talent and achievement throughout my history. It is a ministry of respect that I seek, of affirmation for all that has been as well as for the mysterious that is not yet.

According to Teilhard, the final hallowing of all diminishments, including death, is in seeking to make them a means of communion with God. "Communion through diminishment" is his term. In a splendid conclusion to *The Divine Milieu*, he moves from closely reasoned exposition to the poetry of prayer, as he confronts his own advancing death:

> Grant that I may willingly consent to this last phase of communion in the course of which I shall possess you by diminishing in you.
>
> After having perceived you as the One who is "a greater myself," grant, when my hour comes, that I may recognize you under the species of each alien or hostile force that seems bent upon destroying or uprooting me. When the signs of age begin to mark my body (and still more when they touch my mind); when the ill that is to diminish me or carry me off strikes from without or is born within me; when the

painful moment comes in which I suddenly awaken to the fact that I am ill or growing old; and above all at that last moment when I feel I am losing hold of myself and am absolutely passive within the hands of the great unknown forces that have formed me; in all those dark moments, O God, grant that I may understand that it is you (provided only that my faith is strong enough) who is painfully parting the fibers of my being in order to penetrate to the very marrow of my substance and bear me away within yourself.

This remarkable vision of Teilhard brings the hallowing of our diminishments to its splendid fulfillment.

Tom Ambrogi is a former Jesuit priest (Maryland Province 1947–69) and retired professor, married to a public-interest attorney, Donna Ambrogi; they live at Pilgrim Place, a progressive, ecumenical retirement community in Claremont, California.

A Night Dream Clarifies a Life's Dream

Wilkie Au

I want to share a liberating turning point that occurred in the process of my discerning the question of whether to remain or leave my life as a Jesuit and priest. After four years of prayer and spiritual direction, as well as a year of therapy, I reached a point in 1995 when I felt clear that the next peaceful step in my life was to honor my desire to live a married life. Having sorted out and resolved the many personal issues intertwined in such a major life change, I felt strongly drawn to leave religious life. However, as I lived with this possibility, questions lingered. "How can I make such a decision and still be faithful to God?" I wondered. "Having taken final vows as a Jesuit, how could it be right to leave, with the desire to get married?" It was at this juncture that my unconscious helped me get through an impasse that stumped my conscious mind. It came in the form of what Analytic Psychology calls a "big dream," a dream that has such a big impact that we are never the same afterwards.

The Dream: I was watching a young man saying goodbye to his mother and father, who were weeping and trying to convince him not leave them. But the young man seemed impervious to their sad pleas and remained determined to go off. Witnessing this I found myself angry with the young man for his insensitivity to his parents' pain. Then, in a flash of insight, I realized that I was that young man at nineteen, saying goodbye to my parents in Honolulu to join the Jesuits in California. Then a second scenario quickly followed. I saw myself (then at the age of fifty-one) running down the long flight of stairs of my childhood home, sobbing with grief and heading in the direction of Noreen, my future wife.

My Interpretation: Reflecting on the dream, I came to see its importance in my discernment. This dream provided a perspective that I had not considered. By weaving the two scenarios into one dream, the dream helped me to see a connection between the past and the present. I began to understand that the decision I had made as a young man to enter religious life and the decision I was struggling to make in midlife were rooted in the same desire to be faithful to a call of God that seemed similarly shrouded in mystery. The dream reflected my agnostic Chinese father's angry objection to my going off to live an "unworldly" and celibate life. Somehow, I had possessed the ego strength at nineteen to be undeterred by my father's objections and his threat to sue the Society of Jesus if I were allowed to enter. Just as the dream captured my determination to enter religious life, even if it meant defying a father whom I loved dearly, it also reflected my sadness at leaving the Jesuit order, which had been my home for over thirty years.

The dream helped me realize that the call at age nineteen and at age fifty-one were of one piece: to follow God trustingly into an unknown and scary future that would unfold with God's support. Strengthened by this dream, I later applied for and received a dispensation from my vows, as well as permission to marry in the Church. Since then, I have grown in my belief that a faithful following of God requires that we stay in an ongoing conversation with the God of Easter, who always leads us from dead ends into new highways of possibilities, from deserts of desolation to oases of fresh hope. Our commitment to live faithful lives fails, as James Whitehead puts so well, "not when earlier versions undergo change, but when we can no longer imagine that God is about something in our life." This experience has convinced me of the importance of paying attention to our dreams when discerning. It often happens that when we have exhausted all our conscious efforts to resolve an impasse, a dream comes from the deeper self and the indwelling Presence that shows us the way. Such it was for Joseph who was told in a dream to follow through with his plans to marry Mary, in spite of the complications of a mysterious pregnancy (Mt. 1: 18-22). So it can be for us too, as the God of surprises supports our journey by day and by night.

Wilkie Au (California Province 1963–95) recently retired from Loyola Marymount University. He and his wife, Noreen Cannon, live in Redondo Beach, California.

Transition to Transformation

John A. Baumann, SJ

My life as a Jesuit followed the usual pattern of most Jesuits in California who entered in the mid-1950s. For the first ten years, my formation cultivated in me a perspective of seeing God in all things. It was focused on the immediate, personal interactions within a largely homogeneous Catholic environment: teaching in a Catholic high school, working in the Catholic community, living in Jesuit community.

If life in the Jesuits changed little for me during those ten years, the same was not true for the rest of the world. This was the age of reform and revolution in the country and the church. The civil rights movement, hippie culture, Chicano awareness, anti-war protests, gay recognition, feminist equality, and free speech dominated the headlines. Vatican II, which closed in 1965, quickly exerted influence on how we understood our Church should interact with contemporary society. The following year, the Society of Jesus held its 31st General Congregation, and its declarations about "the faith that does justice" unleashed our imaginations.

In 1966, during my first year of theology, our Jesuit Provincial committed the province to initiate several new apostolates, one of which was for social ministries. The next year, 1967, Jesuit Father General Pedro Arrupe wrote a letter on Race Relations in the U. S. and encouraged Jesuits to respond to the crisis in that area. With a commitment from the province to allow Jesuits to go into social ministry, and the challenge of Vatican II and our general Congregation to react appropriately, I took the opportunity to explore a social ministries apostolate.

Transition to Transformation

After some arm twisting with superiors I headed off to Chicago for the summer of 1967, before my second year of theology studies, to attend the Urban Training Center. The Urban Training Center was created in the 1960s for the purpose of training clergy and laity to relate the program of the churches to the critical needs of the inner cities. During the first of three months, we were introduced to Saul Alinsky, who is generally considered to be the founder of modern community organizing. His model of organizing focused on improving the living conditions of poor communities across the country. During the final two months, I did field placement in a community organization on the West Side of Chicago under the direction of Tom Gaudette, an Alinsky lieutenant and key figure in the field of community organizing in the United States. That summer in Chicago became the life-changing first step toward the adventure that has been the rest of my life.

When I returned to theology for my second year, my studies came alive for me. Theology was no longer an abstraction; it became concrete and personal. My faith had been transformed and theology gave me a way to think about my summer experience. Theology is about putting gospel values into action. I began to understand better the Ignatian spirituality that God is present in our world and active in our lives. If we believe that God is among us, how can we allow divisions based on ethnicity, religion, or background to create animosity, injustice, or violence? I better understood the meaning of becoming a contemplative in action. I began to see that it means allowing God to flow into my relationship with people. It is about the core values of the Gospel—justice, integrity, love, hope, healing, compassion, and service. It is about Faith that does Justice. It is about a life of service to

John A. Baumann, SJ

others to work for justice and the common good that stems from the dignity, unity, and equality of all people; every aspect of social life must be related to faith in order for it to attain its fullest meaning.

After ordination in 1969, I returned to Chicago for more training in community organizing, and in 1972 I co-founded PICO (People Improving Communities through Organizing), a national and international network of faith-based community organizations.

In 2012 we celebrated PICO's 40th anniversary. Taking a cue from what Jesus says to Nicodemus in John's Gospel about the Spirit allowing us to be born again, starting PICO was also a kind of birthday for me, for working with PICO has opened me to a faith that is receptive to how this spirit is at work in organizing people in the midst of the hardest challenges society faces. PICO's aspiration and mission is to continue to serve a network of congregation- and faith-based organizations to assist in the building of community organizations with the power to improve the quality of life of families and neighborhoods.

John Baumann, SJ, entered the California Province in 1956. He is co-founder of the PICO National Network, a model of faith-based community organizing. He is director of special projects for PICO, and continues to work on justice and peace issues in California, Central America, and Rwanda. He has attended all but two Compañeros reunions since 1994 and often leads the Eucharistic celebration at those meetings.

Still a Jesuit, transformed

Spiritual Change in Personal History

Eugene C. Bianchi

It's hard to write about changes in spirituality over a life cycle for at least two reasons. I'm no longer the teenager of the 1940s in an Italian-American community in Oakland, California. As a university professor of religion, I have criticized the pre-Vatican II Church over a long period. So I should take special care not to neglect the good-enough aspects of religion in that era, just as I should cherish good-enough parents, extended family, and nuns who taught me. This brings up the second difficulty. One's "religion" or spirituality is a subtle amalgam of the secular and the formally religious. Experiencing love from my mother and uncle was more important in spiritual development than Saturday confession and Sunday Mass.

I entered the Society of Jesus after graduating from a Jesuit high school in 1948. Our early training was both isolated and rule-bound. I had relatively little experience of the wider world except for part-time jobs. I, like most entrants, was sexually inexperienced. Religious practices in the order gave me an early grounding in Christian spirituality, but they did not deeply penetrate my life. Friendships with fellow classmates, some to last a lifetime, were the human-spiritual bonds of staying a Jesuit. My years of studying theology in Louvain before ordination began to open new doors as the church prepared for Vatican II.

This broadening of outlook continued in doctoral study at Union Theological Seminary and Columbia University. The combination of Vatican II and the Union-Columbia period, while living with the *America* magazine community, opened me to new freedom and possibility. I sometime wonder how my life would have gone had I not been blessed by these happenings.

After twenty years, I left the Jesuits to teach religious studies at Emory University. In this longest career period of my life, various aspects stand out as seminal for my spirituality. Marriage and failure in marriage taught me lessons of self-awareness, close contact with women, and what it felt like to suffer and to be happy. This was and is a key school of my spiritual learning. These hard relationship experiences also drew me into Jungian therapy and modern psychologies that influenced my teaching and writing. Emory also gave me opportunity to delve into Buddhist and Daoist spirituality, not only for teaching but also for incorporating into practice. I learned tai chi and some yoga and still do them daily. The modern quest for the historical Jesus was also crucial for showing me how much cultural conditioning affects not only scripture but also development of religion and theology. With these freeing insights, lots of things became unstuck for me. I have a more human and less divine understanding of Jesus. I also realized that church structures and teachings could change in important ways. I also felt at ease drawing from many spiritual traditions, East and West, to nourish my spirituality.

From my first article published in a national magazine in 1955, I've cultivated a writer's life. I've written books and other essays on religion and on creative aging. In more recent years, I've had fun doing two novels and a memoir. Now I enjoy writing poems that are special ways of expressing spirituality. Poetry has also drawn me closer to nature, which is a primordial spiritual source. I live on the Oconee River in Athens, Georgia, surrounded by a wonderful garden. Those spiritual teachers, our dogs and cats, have been very important parts of our home life. My wife, Peggy Herrman, is a very deep part of my soul's journey.

So Spirit is all around us, within and without. I'll end with a few quotes from Anthony de Mello's *One Minute Wisdom* that make great sense to me in late life. "'Don't look for God,' the Master said. 'Just look and all will be revealed.'" Yet it helps greatly to cultivate meditative solitude: "All suffering comes from a person's inability to sit still and be alone." And finally in keeping with a Jesuit motto, "The master always frowned on anything that seemed sensational. The divine, he claimed, is only found in the ordinary."

For more on all this, please see my web site: http://www.bianchibooks.com

Gene Bianchi (California Province 1948–68) is Professor of Religion Emeritus at Emory University. He was the first director of Emory's Emeritus College from 2001-2008. With Peter McDonough he authored Passionate Uncertainty: Inside the American Jesuits *(2002). Bianchi was in the California Province of the Jesuit order for twenty years, 1948–68. He has published two novels:* The Bishop of San Francisco: Romance, Intrigue and Religion *(2005) and* The Children's Crusade: Scandal at the Vatican *(2008). His writings on the spirituality of aging include:* Aging As a Spiritual Journey *(1982),* On Growing Older *(1985), and* Elder Wisdom: Crafting Your Own Elderhood *(1994). He recently published a memoir,* Taking a Long Road Home *(2011 and a book of poetry,* Ear to the Ground: Poems from the Long View *(2013). He makes his home in Athens, Georgia, with his wife, Margaret (Peggy) Herrman.*

From the Ground Up

William J. Bichsel, SJ

I am honored that Don Foran asked me to write a brief life-sketch for this book. As I write this on November 3, 2013, it is the fourth anniversary of the "Disarm Now Plowshares" action in which I was one of five who cut through the fences to gain entry into the nuclear weapons storage area at the US Trident submarine base at Bangor, Washington. This area is known as SWF-PAC (Strategic Weapons Facility Pacific) and holds close to one fourth of our nation's nuclear weapons, which are fitted onto missiles carried by Trident subs. Those taking part with me were: Sr. Ann Montgomery, RSCJ, (now deceased), Susan Crane, Lynne Greenwald, and Steve Kelly, SJ. By our action we wanted to shout out to all of our Northwest neighbors (and to our nation) that these harbingers of death are in our backyard. We wanted to sound an alarm that if we, the people of the Northwest, don't take leadership toward abolishing these weapons, who will?

Once inside that graveyard of hopelessness, we were cuffed by Marines carrying assault rifles, hooded with some sort of sack, and made to lie facedown on the ground for three hours.

During that time, we five experienced a great surge of joy. We had entered the Valley of Death and were alive and full of joy.

For the thirty-five years that I have been resisting the presence of the Trident submarines and their lethal load at Bangor, Washington. I have had the inner desire to stand inside this area where the weapons are stored, and stand there as a believer and witness to the Resurrection. Jesus would be there where the danger and threat of death is. His presence is stronger than nuclear weapons and his power of

Resurrection is able to transform hearts addicted to nuclear weapons into hearts of human compassion. In the power of the Resurrection those instruments of death can be hammered into plowshares to serve human beings. Lying hooded on the ground, my companions and I experienced a joy that can only come from a freedom-loving, compassionate God.

Along with Gilberto Perez, a Buddhist monk, I have recently returned from the South Korean island of Jeju where the United States is building a navy base that the villagers of the island are resisting. At the heart of the resistance is the Eucharist, which is celebrated every day on the side of the main road across from one of the entrance gates to the ongoing construction site. The blocking is being done by priests, nuns, and the villagers of Gangjeong. The inspiration for the Eucharistic resistance is Bishop Peter Chang, a gentle man who is strong in his belief that Jesus walks where people are hurting and where the danger is. Four Korean Jesuit priests have been assigned by the Korean Provincial to support the villagers and the ongoing resistance. Two of the Jesuits are currently in jail for their work. Never have I been more proud of the Jesuits, whose entire province is strongly behind the resistance.

My experience of Jeju has brought me the deepest joy I have ever experienced of a faith community in total resistance to US forces of militarism. I do believe that this experience of deep joy has given direction to my life. I also believe that though the resisters feel very small and insignificant, I experienced a depth of spirituality on Jeju that I believe can be the deep well of grace from which people can draw, not only to stop the construction of the base but also to roll back American militarism in the Pacific.

We as church are invited and urged to join in their blessed resistance and become the presence of Jesus in our world. We stand in need of their spirit of resistance to the forces of destruction over the long haul.

I am the product of a working-class Catholic family with six boys and one girl, Mary Theresa, who was the youngest of the children. My dad was a railroad engineer and was elected local and then national chairman of the Brotherhood of Locomotive Engineers on the Northern Pacific. My mother was Irish in blood and wit and fed the guys coming up from the tracks to our back porch, where she had set up a table and four chairs. One problem I had as a youngster was that she would feed the ones from the tracks with bacon or ham on Fridays. I tried to warn her that she was imperiling her soul by serving meat on Fridays. She replied that God knows best and she continued on this dangerous path.

My family is the ground or the Prime Matter out of which I grew. Coming out of my familial ground I was set upon the course of meeting those who would influence and help shape me. I think I am a composite of those whom I met and with whom I interacted in my teens and early years. Dutch Schultz, Jim Flannery, Paul Robinson, Larry Donohue, and Jack O'Leary influenced me greatly. They each had gifts that I longed for but didn't have. These also entered the Jesuits as I did. As a matter of fact, as he returned to Bellarmine High School after being in the navy during WWII, Larry Donohue led me into the Jesuits.

After entering the Jesuits with the aforementioned, I met and was influenced by Gus Schneider, Rock Rekofke, Dave Freitag, and Tom Greif—among others. I feel that what I have become and what I have done in working for social justice would not have been possible without them. Over time all but Rock Rekofke, Jack O'Leary, and I had left the Jesuits. Certainly, the others maintain their Jesuit connection. Years ago when I was with a group of ex-Jesuits and some Jesuits, some of the ex-Jesuits expressed feelings of guilt at having left. I told them I made up for that by my feeling of guilt for having stayed. Now I'm good with it.

Within me there is this double sense of bringing my companions with me to some action or event and of being sent by my companions to do a certain action or take part in an event.

This feeling came home to me strongly in 1996 when Br. Fred Mercy, SJ, and I were sent to the Federal Prison at Sheridan, Oregon, for trespassing at the School of the Americas at Fort Benning, Georgia. That year was the fiftieth anniversary of my entering the Order in 1946—at Sheridan, Oregon. As I walked around the prison track I could see the old Jesuit novitiate building sitting high on a distant hill. I sensed the difference between the two institutional buildings. But above anything I felt a comic approval of my being there by my companions. All of them had also entered the Jesuit Order at Sheridan and did their time there as well. I still experience a deep rootedness with my companions—deceased or alive—that gives sense and direction to my journey.

Along with my companions mentioned, I'm deeply thankful for Joanie Bartello who has taught me love for the long haul, and for other significant women such as Gloria Kidd who have been life teachers for me. In closing I give deep thanks to my G Street, Guadalupe, St. Leo, Catholic Worker community and people like Joe and Theresa Power-Drutis who have put up with me and have been the nourishing topsoil for my growth and sustained action.

Bill "Bix" Bichsel, SJ, entered the Oregon Province of the Jesuits in 1946 and has for many years been a pastoral minister and member of the Catholic Worker community in Tacoma, Washington.

Broadcasting, Religious Life, & Unpredictable Graces

James A. Brown

I grew up in Cleveland fascinated with radio—both listening and, while in high school, as volunteer announcer and actor on educational FM programs broadcast to the city's public school classrooms. Radio was in my blood. Then in the late 1940s along came television—at the same time that I was wondering what my future life should be. After a senior retreat I decided to pass on the broadcasting interests and move to a different challenge: joining the Jesuits.

I relished the quiet time for reflection and liturgy, the exciting chance to join in sports for the first time with fellow seminarians, and to move on into academic studies in future years. All those years of early religious training coupled with collegiate-level courses surprisingly also offered occasions to write about and to put together recorded programs, not unlike radio. Instead of going directly to regency high- school teaching, the regional director of studies had me go instead to the University of Detroit, where they were introducing a complete series of freshman courses over the newly established city-wide "educational TV" (aka, later, public broadcasting) station. Within months I was producing and directing almost ten live half-hour broadcasts a week. After one year my superiors said that the college needed a Jesuit to chair the department of radio-TV, so I should find a university that offered a doctorate in related studies. That brought me to the University of Southern California to pursue its degree, with residence for five years at Loyola High School in Los Angeles.

I had much interaction with major personnel in the motion picture and television industry there, and active mentoring of handfuls of Loyola students. Having a flexible schedule, I was able to substitute for scholastics' classes in almost every discipline except chemistry—my only formal contact with the high-schoolers. Throughout this stimulating period I continued to find religious life significant and satisfying.

I moved on to theology and thrived at first. I was happy to be back among others doing the same thing as I. But by then, Vatican II was in process, and my colleagues were exploring many new paths. I still felt strong attraction to our traditional form of religious life and became increasingly perplexed and distressed as others experimented and adapted their living styles and procedures. For more than a year I was confused and hurt to the point of serious depression—possibly not far from some sort of breakdown. But with supportive superiors I gradually worked through this and emerged with a more open attitude to changes in religious life. But still I embraced basic belief and personal prayer-life.

After ordination I was assigned back to U. of Detroit to head the small Radio-TV academic department. There I flourished, sometimes teaching four or five courses every semester while chairing, plus extra-curriculars and broadcast production work. And I loved directing retreats, mostly to laymen and college students. Twice I directed 8-day retreats for province scholastics in studies there. But I wore out with the frantic 12-hour days, yet remained mostly faithful to religious meditation, prayer, reading, and sacraments. The large group of Jesuit faculty in the residence was congenial and supportive, but I was something of a loner in my peripheral field of broadcasting.

A series of administrative contretemps along with my fatigue led me to seek alternative work at the end of a 7-month tertianship. I arranged a one-year resident consultant position with a friend from Los Angeles who had become CBS Television Network president in New York City. That went well, with residence at Nativity Parish around the corner from Dorothy Day's Catholic Worker. Spiritual life continued strong during those months in Manhattan.

Then I was sought by the University of Southern California chairman to join his faculty in the Telecommunications Department where I had earned my PhD. This time I lived at Loyola Marymount University while commuting to the USC campus. I also gave occasional retreats to laymen.

At a meeting in Santa Barbara of Jesuits in communication, I commented that through the years I had lived pretty much alone in my somewhat marginal area of communications. Afterwards a young Jesuit came to my room and we shared our mutual interests. We kept in touch, mostly by letters, until he finished theology and joined the faculty at Loyola Marymount, where we became close friends and colleagues in media-related work. Personally this was the first time in my life I had bonded closely with another person! It was exhilarating. We enjoyed work-related activities, swimming, campus liturgies, co-directing lay retreats. A sudden major disruption in his life devastated me for months as we severed contact; that was the second time I skirted a nervous or emotional breakdown.

Struggling through this crushing inter-personal rupture, I discovered gentle and warm support (that word again!) from a youngish woman in our work area. This led to an extended affair that brought healing and some form of peace. But it was a contradiction to my religious commitment, and eventually I chose to leave the Society of Jesus, intending to marry. My Midwest provincial's positive response to my telling him this was: "I don't look to the Church's or the Society's 'success' as to how many institutions we run or how many men we have, but rather that we each keep open to the continuing mystery of God in our lives." Then we both went down to the snack room and chatted over beers.

My female friend and I never married but have continued to be best friends to this day. I left teaching at USC and for a year commuted to New York as a program consultant to the President/CEO of corporate CBS, Inc. Without the structure and formalities of a religious community, I continued with the Church's liturgy and informal prayer. Then I returned to USC at a higher rank in a related department for several years until, despite publishing a book on broadcast management used at 108 colleges and many scholarly articles, I did not receive tenure.

Fortunately, the University of Alabama recruited me to head their larger department, so I moved from L.A. after almost a quarter century there. This was clearly a fortuitous move, for the administration, faculty, and students were a joy to be with, and the Catholic parish on campus was a vibrant community of students, faculty, and football players and coaches. I continued close to prayer and sacraments, while embracing progressive Vatican II principles. My broadcast activities continued too. Life was good. I enjoyed a series of faithful dogs, a growing circle of friends, and contact with former students from Detroit, USC, and Loyola Marymount. In the meantime my young close Jesuit friend of yore and I had reconnected and resumed a long-distance but deep friendship—my serving as his best man at his wedding (as I had once concelebrated his first Mass with him).

It was about this time, in my mid-60s, that I came to the gradual realization that my previous neutral interest in women and my closer friendship with men led me to a late-in-life realization that I was homosexual in orientation (a slow learner indeed!). Through friends, some former Jesuits, I came in contact with groups and national organizations that delicately opened up for me new avenues of self-awareness and activity. After retiring a decade ago, I moved to Atlanta to join a partner, and we oversaw construction of our new house. After three years, however, we parted but remain very close friends. The past decade and a half have been a revelation and a fulfilling time—all still in the context of active Catholic involvement in a local parish, comprised mostly of blacks and Hispanics, where I am chaplain of the men's fraternal group. Personal prayer is stronger and richer than ever.

So, life is good, God is good. I close reflecting on eternity. Since life has been a blessing, I suspect the best is yet to come.

Jim "TV" Brown (Detroit Province 1950–77) travels west and north of Atlanta from time to time and sometimes to Guatemala to visit the families of five young men he has sponsored for various lengths of time over the past decade.

An Unexpected Patriarch

Edward L. Burke

By the time you read this, I'll be ninety years old, God willing. Let me tell you about a recent notable turning point in my life.

(First I should mention that, for me, context, which is necessary to fully understand any event, is three-dimensional. It goes back in time. So, sit back and let me tell you a three-dimensional tale.)

My parents were both born in San Francisco, toward the end of the 19th century. They came from distinctly different parts of "the City." My mother came from the still flourishing Italian quarter, which the natives refer to as "North Beach." Her father ran a winery and saloon. My father, on the other hand, came from "South of Market," a less affluent, industrialized neighborhood, largely inhabited by Irish immigrants. His father was a teamster, which in those days meant that he drove a team of horses. Basically, he was a truck driver before there were trucks.

Neither of my parents had an easy upbringing. My mothers' mother died on Christmas Eve, at the age of thirty-one, when my mother was nine years old. Four months later, she and her two siblings were literally thrown out of bed by the San Francisco earthquake. My parents always referred to that event as "the Fire," rather than "the Earthquake." Among other things, the fire destroyed her father's winery. Then there was the First World War. Then the Great Flu. Then the Depression.

Fortunately my mother had an aunt, her mother's older sister, with no children of her own, who stepped in. She was the only grandmother I ever knew. Her English wasn't perfect, but she used to sing "Fa la nana" to put me to sleep, and I thought she was the world's greatest cook.

An Unexpected Patriarch

My father's parents did not have a happy marriage. It was punctuated with drinking and violence. The Irish Catholic version of divorce in those days was simply to live apart, which my grandparents did off and on over a period of years.

My father was small for his age, but he was "tough." I recall his telling me that he used to go out walking around his neighborhood looking for a fight. That was the purpose of the walk. It didn't matter much with whom. Occasionally he would come home with a black eye. In that case, his father would give him a beating for having gotten into the fight.

Dad avoided school when he could. He could easily elude his maternal grandfather, assigned to follow him at half a block's distance to see that he got there. Once free, Dad headed for the nearby railroad yards. As freight trains entered from the South, headed for the Townsend St. Station, they gradually slowed down their speed. Dad and his friends would start running parallel to the freight car, until they were going at the same speed. Then they would bend down and run diagonally under the train and come out on the other side, if they were successful. One of his friends lost a leg.

No doubt about it. My father had the makings of a juvenile delinquent. But then things changed. Enter Mr. Sydney Peixotto and the Columbia Park Boys Club (CPBC). Mr. Peixotto's cure for the juvenile delinquent? Give him something better to do.

He was a master organizer and fundraiser but, more importantly, he knew how to connect with teenagers. I remember my father's telling me how he first became interested in joining the CPBC. When they played baseball (his passion), they had uniforms! And that wasn't all they had. They had a band (also with uniforms). My Dad learned to play the trombone.

And they went on trips! Mr. Peixotto's way of getting the boys out of the City during the summer, during which they had too much free time and too little focus, was to take them—about 30 of them—on a walking trip along El Camino Real (before it was paved) to Los Angeles!

I grew up hearing my father tell of the adventures he had with the CPBC. And his stories were full of "Mr. Peixotto used to say . . . Mr. Peixotto said once . . . Mr. Peixotto always said . . ." He almost never mentioned his own father.

I never met Mr. Peixotto. He died when I was only a couple of years old. But he was my Jewish grandfather, and I'm proud of him. There's a public playground in San Francisco named after him. I owe him. In imitation of him my father dedicated his own life to teaching physical education to kids.

Summary of my account so far: My mother was largely raised by a woman who was not her birth mother, and my father was formed morally and physically by a man who was not his natural father. Those ancestors have made me who I am today.

And what of the turning point in my life? God has given me good health. Though I was the oldest, I survived both my siblings as well as their respective spouses. As a result, I have unexpectedly inherited eight children and thirteen grandchildren, the grandchildren currently being in their late twenties and early thirties.

The realization dawned on me at a family gathering organized by one of my nieces five years ago. Her son, a member of the 101st Airborne, was about to be sent overseas to Afghanistan, and she wanted all the cousins to get together before he left. Many (including me) had not seen one another for many years.

I found myself seated at the end of a table, with several of both younger generations. The conversation was initially awkward and soon reached a lull. I had the feeling that the others were waiting for me to say something. At the same time, I didn't feel I had anything special to say. So I waited too. Then one of the younger grandsons, in college at the time, (probably the

An Unexpected Patriarch

sharpest of the lot, but one I would want to watch closely) walked up to the other end of the table, immediately sized up the situation and said, "Come on, Uncle Ed, say something wise!" I replied, "That's just the feeling I have, Quinn. I have the feeling that people are waiting for me to say something special, and I don't have anything special to say." That broke the ice, and we all got around to talking about the stuff and things of our lives.

When the party was over, we all gathered for a big photograph of the whole family. I was seated in the center, though I had begotten none of them. What I have realized since (and the awareness has grown) is that I had become a patriarch! And I love it!

Since then I have taken a new interest in all their doings. Many of them have been involved with attending college, which my academic background allows me to relate to. Some of them have needed financial help, and I have tried to do what I could to prevent them from finishing their education with a debt looming over their heads. Others are preparing to get married.

Need I say that my own life has been extraordinarily enriched by this newfound role in their lives? Each one is different. Some are closer, some more needy than others. I'm not there to tell them what to do. They have their own lives to live. My role, as I see it, is to be there for them in whatever way I can.

Looking back on the lives of my parents and my own history, I am struck by this role of the unexpected mentor, parent, etc., and I'm grateful to be part of such a process.

Ed Burke was in the California Province from 1942 to 1968. He is Professor of Clinical Psychology Emeritus at UCSF, and has lived in Larkspur, California, for many years. Besides being his family's patriarch, Ed is one of our two beloved nonagenarian Compañeros.

One Life

Morgan Zo Callahan

When I was a boy, I felt, especially in nature, the presence of a "greater-than-I," a mysterious creative power, the source of love, life and wonder. Gazing into the stars at night or viewing perfectly blue skies, I felt reverence for God and gratitude for being alive. But religion at times was another matter; my adopted Irish American family and religious culture brought gifts but also inculcated a fear of a God as a moralistic judge. Some of the nuns yelled that my sinful actions hurt Jesus himself. I had disturbing dreams of the Irish priests preaching about the fires of hell. In contrast, I loved the music and sense of prayerfulness encouraged in the church, such as Masses with Gregorian chanting or quiet moments. In my early teens, though I would never dare to say it, I became angry at the God who sat in judgment, favoring some, annihilating others. When I went to the university, I wondered if my conceptions of self as a separate soul or entity and God as a personal, parental, all-powerful being were flawed. Is, as Buckminster Fuller surmises, God a verb rather than a noun? Could the idea of God as a judge that controls all, rewarding and condemning, be wrong?

In 1961 I was a high-school junior, boarding as a student-worker at Loyola High School in Los Angeles. During the summer and some weekends, I would hitchhike around L.A., not always having a definite destination in mind: Venice Beach, downtown, Hollywood & Vine, the Farmer's Market, the San Fernando Valley, and the Fairfax District. Once, just above the frenetic 101 freeway, I was attracted to an Indian Vedanta temple, the Hollywood Hills' miniature version of the Taj

Mahal. On a bright, blue-sky day, the Southern California sun shone on the yellow domes of the white, gold-spired temple. Built in 1938 by the Vedanta Society of Southern California, it drew Westerners interested in Eastern mysticism, including literary luminaries Aldous Huxley and Christopher Isherwood. Inside the temple, I contemplated an artistic depiction of Buddha's round face, peaceful and tender, across from the Shroud of Turin's image of Jesus. I just sat there, a bit uncomfortable at first, and then more relaxed, enjoying the still sanctuary. On subsequent visits, I could slow down, reflect, and escape the ordinary anxieties of a high-school student.

In 1970, I spent a sweaty summer in Chicago to train as a "Saul Alinsky" community organizer. Guru-founder of modern community organizing, author of *Reveille for Radicals* (1946), Chicagoan son of Russian Jewish immigrant parents, Saul Alinsky (1909–72) was dedicated to improving housing and working conditions in poor communities such as Chicago's Back of the Yards neighborhood

During my training in Chicago, one of our teams organized apartment residents—mostly immigrants from Mexico and Central America who were living in slum conditions. The landlord procrastinated in the repair of lead-painted peeling walls, broken plumbing, and pest infestation. Some children suffered lead poisoning by ingesting paint chips from the walls. The strong conviction and united energy of the tenants provided the engine for us to form a base of solidarity: meetings, educational and artistic presentations, and social events such as potluck dinners and a dance with live music. Alinsky writes, "A good tactic is one the people enjoy."

The 1968 Democratic Convention was fresh in the minds of Chicagoans. Americans watched TV scenes of police and National Guard beating yippies, hippies, students, assorted protesters, poets, and activists. In the summer of 1970, protests, especially against the Vietnam War, spread throughout Chicago and many US cities. Our venture was a needle in the haystack of discontent with the system, but it was still worthwhile because it was generated from a determined community, a community developed around a cause: all people cherish a safe, clean home.

In July 1998, Bob Holstein gathered a small group of men to do the Spiritual Exercises under the direction of Don Merrifield, SJ, in the long form that is described in the Nineteenth Annotation of Ignatius's final text. Don said it would be fine to start without preconceptions of a theistic / creator / original-sin theology. We did the "four weeks" over thirty-four weeks with some spiritual direction available and some group meeting at Loyola Marymount University.

I contemplated Jesus's appeal for us to love each other, even the most down and out, contemplating Jesus in prison, in the hospital, living on the street. I examined my conscience each day, observing mind, body, feelings, and emotions. Unlike in my earlier years, I did not feel shame and sorrow that Jesus suffered. I acknowledged my responsibility to help those suffering in our own time, those Jesus said represent his presence on earth: the oppressed, the poor, the abused children, the hungry and cold, the forgotten people. I prayed for my family, friends, students and co-workers. I forgave other people while asking for forgiveness, for a good sense of humor, and for patience.

I enjoyed moments of solitude and comments by fellow retreatants. Bob Brophy expressed our orientation well: "A clear difference between our present perceptions and those of Ignatius's day is the demand that we de-center mankind—we have lost confidence that humans are the unique purpose of the cosmos. . . . All this is God's goodness exploding in beauty."

I noticed similarities between Ignatius and the Buddha. The onset of the Buddha's spiritual crisis is told in a story. At dawn in the palace of Gautama, after a night of revelry, the rich prince, admired and accomplished, notices the unattractive sleeping poses and sounds of the beautiful women who had been dancing for his enjoyment just few hours earlier. He sees through the enchantments of the evening. Both Iñigo and the Buddha gave up a privileged life and immersed themselves in a quest for peace and happiness, realizing the Source of life within human joys and sorrows. Christ, as Gerard Manley Hopkins, SJ, says, "plays in ten thousand places."

Morgan Zo Callahan (California Province 1962–71) and his spouse Doris Chang Callahan live in Temple City, California. He has published Intimate Meanderings *and, most recently,* Bamboo Bending: An Educator's Changing Corner of the Universe.

My Many Lives

L. Patrick Carroll

I was not well during my final two years in the Jesuits. I had suffered a cardiac arrest and gone directly back to work. At St. Aloysius, in Spokane, I frequently did four Masses on a weekend, and then spent three days recovering. I played a lot of golf, and I worked less than I ever had, but I still was tired all the time. I experienced frequent cardiac arrests usually when asleep, though my defibrillator quickly revived me. The fright level and psychological disturbance were far greater than I was acknowledging.

I was drinking too much, sleeping too little, making choices that were not the best for me or for others. Put simply, my life fell apart, spiritually and psychologically. Quietly, one Sunday morning, at the Provincial's insistence, I left my St. Aloysius ministry. After three months of counseling and prayer, I went on a leave of absence from the Society of Jesus and, eventually, from the active priestly ministry.

I loved my years as parish priest. I believe deeply in the possibility of the local church, no matter how dysfunctional the larger diocesan or universal church might be. We need a community to support individual belief, a place and a people with whom to gather for moments of great joy or pain, a vision larger than ourselves to challenge us to be our best and truest, our most gospel-centered self. No one is an island, sufficient to themselves. No one, finally, believes alone.

I remain a parishioner today—at St. Joseph's Church in Seattle where I grew up and at which I twice served as a priest.

In the fall of 1998, when, in great pain and with tremendous trepidation, I took a leave of absence from the Jesuits, I was no longer part of the dynamic Jesuit community that I'd been in for forty-four years and ordained a priest for more than thirty-one. Actions of the past, my health, my very history of having worked in every part of our province caught up with me. I could see no alternative except, at sixty-two years of age, to begin life anew.

The departure was most painful. A poem I posted on the bulletin board on that November morning, just before I drove away from the Jesuit Provincial residence, captured my feelings then:

Who Am I Now?

All these years of knowing who I am
by how I signed myself.
How strange that space,
there, after my name,
blank, bland, empty.

At first we signed it little: n.s.j.
Novices, beginners, small case.
How proud to put S.J., there
telling the world to whom it was that
I belonged.
Books by me, S.J.;
Articles by me, S.J.;
Countless letters
To editors, friends, enemies,
And other companions,
Telling what I believed,
what I was about,
not just by text,
but how I signed myself—

L. Patrick Carroll

Proudly, easily,
Lazily,
Sometimes dishonestly,
Society of Jesus.

I stare at my name today
and wonder, as I will in days ahead,
Who am I
and who will I become?
To whom can I belong,
what company, companionship, society
If not Jesus?
I just can't tell the world—each time,
can't remind myself—each time.
It has to be inside,
as all along
I've wanted it to be,
in the society of Jesus.

Pat Carroll (Oregon Province 1954–98) has spent a full life in the Jesuits and since he left. He and his spouse, Dee McQuesten, live in Seattle, Washington. Among Pat's books of poems and memoirs and spirituality texts are A Crooked Finger Beckons *(2002) and* The Right Place for Love: Memories in Interesting Times. *Pat presided over the first Jesuit co-ed high school (Bellarmine Prep in Tacoma, Washington), and the first program offering Ignatian Spiritual Exercises to lay people, led by laity. He also authored the Introduction to this book.*

Deciding Times

Gary Chamberlain

Spring 1966, last months of regency teaching *The Aeneid* to seniors and American Studies to sophomores at St. Louis U. High. Suddenly—letter from Rome: next assignment, not to St. Mary's, Kansas, with the rest of my class for theology but to the JAPAN MISSION! Now where did that come from? Seems that in the fervor and fever of the novitiate I had volunteered for the African mission; then I forgot all about it. But someone picked up on it!

Since I was finishing my classes for a Master's in constitutional law at U. of Chicago, I requested a delay until I could write my thesis, finishing AND defending in early 1967. After another Chicago study and end of classes, I returned to stay at St. Louis U., Duborg Hall, the Jesuit residence.

And there and then it happened one fateful August day—a friend from Denver, Sharon Keller, arrived with a friend of hers, Sharon Demong, and asked my help in finding an apartment. I can still see the scene as I walked down the Duborg steps on Grand Blvd. to their waiting car and met the new Sharon. In the coming weeks, I helped them find a place near Washington U. I worked on the thesis (a study of the Supreme Court's recent Miranda ruling), helped out the SLU debate team, coached and traveled to tournaments with them, and took up Japanese language classes at Washington U. Nice coincidence that I could drop by the Sharons' apartment close by after my weekly class, have tea and conversation. Gradually noticed that signs appeared on the apartment door with Japanese characters; only later did I realize that Sharon D. was doing that.

Christmas 1966—back in Denver. I see Sharon over the holidays at a party. Early January—thesis work at SLU; I visit Sharon at her apartment after more Japanese classes at WU and see her at friends' places. A trip to Chicago for thesis defense; preparation for trip to Japan complete (my trunk with all my clothes sent over). Ready to leave but am taking the February to travel from St. Louis to St. Mary's, Kansas (by bus); Denver (train), San Antonio (bus), Albuquerque, and finally L.A. and LAX. The night before I leave St. Louis, friends are going to throw a party for me, take me to dinner. Sharon's invited. That day I ask Sharon D. if I can borrow her VW bug to visit friends around St. Louis to say good-bye. For all I know this will be it for the rest of my life!

When I return the car and she drops me off, Sharon says with some force, "You shouldn't give people the impression you're available!" Well, that set my brain afire! So at dinner that night I look at her with new interest. But next day I'm off on the bus with a small sendoff group, including Sharon.

Along the way of my journeys toward L.A., some seeds have been planted, and my cross-country journey turns into a persistent meditation on my own identity. I had always been identified by others, including most recently the Jesuits, and I needed to have a "family" after parental divorce at age three. The young Jesuit scholastics had attracted me to the Society. Yet, I began to realize during regency at SLUH, I enjoyed being with my students and their families more than the Jesuit community. I saw a wholeness in the families I had not seen in my own. AND I felt accepted for who I AM, not because I was a good student, good novice, etc. I start to explore this decision to go to Japan and asked if I really wanted this for myself. Then, of course, there was this attractive, engaging woman in St. Louis who seemed interested in me. What a cocktail.

I arrive in Denver and visit Sharon's family to say farewell. As I leave, her mother says, "If you ever leave the Jesuits, look Sharon up." Sharon's brother just about drops his jaw on the floor. I keep going and end up in L.A. with my Dad and stepmother Sallye for my last few days. I am in a church a lot, just thinking, praying, churning....

What do I want to do? Who am I at this point in my life? Up to now I had lived thinking I was pleasing Father, heavenly, earthly, Holy, and Jesuits. I had written Sharon a "nice-to-know-you; see you when I return after ordination" letter, and so thought I had put all that behind me. But...

Finally, a decision emerges: on to Japan, but I call Sharon. It's Wednesday or Thursday before I leave. 5:00 a.m. L.A. time. I make the call. Not sure what all I did say, but out came the words, "I'm 99 and 44/100% sure I love you, but I'm off to Japan." Hang up. Dad comes into the hall, with the words, "You didn't have to get up this early for our golf game." I just murmur something, and we are off for 18 holes.

End of ninth hole back at the clubhouse, "Call for Gary Chamberlain." Now that is interesting. It's my stepmother informing me that a young woman from St. Louis wants me to call her right away. That is a lot more exciting than my golf score.

The call goes through. Sharon' simple question: "If you really love me, why are you going to Japan?" This knocks my socks off, golf shoes and all! That was it, the deciding moment. Three realities came together, Trinitarian form: I was not going to Japan; I was going to leave the Jesuits; and I was going to marry Sharon Demong! Of course, that last point would have to wait. Meanwhile, Dad is not just impatient at holding up the game but very curious. So back at the house I explain the whole "churning" process of the past month and my decisions (or was there just one momentous decision?). He's happy, but then there's the farewell party two days away, not to mention my Japan-bound luggage.

I figure I had better let the Provincial back in St. Louis know. I call, and they think I am calling from Tokyo. I assure them that I am in L.A. and deliver the news of my decision, MINUS part 3 about a woman in St. Louis. Well, can't just leave; "need time for reflection, etc." So I am sent to Rockhurst College, Kansas City, to weigh my decision. Great, since that's an easy four-hour drive for Sharon to cross the state for a weekend visit.

And the rest is pretty much history. Mother is happy; Grandmother Thomson is disappointed. I am ecstatic! A Jesuit at Rockhurst lines me up with a job teaching philosophy at St. Benedict's College, Atchison, Kansas, and Sharon and I carry on our romantic relationship. Cut to the chase: married June 15, 1968 and still am in 2014.

Gary Chamberlain (Missouri Province 1956–67) joined the theology faculty at Seattle University in 1979 and retired in 2009. He recently published a book, Troubled Water: Religion, Ethics, and the Global Water Crisis.

A Jesuit Journey

John F. Christensen

The day that John F. Kennedy was assassinated, I was a first year novice at Los Gatos in the middle of the long retreat. This dark event in American history, and in my young adult life, was brought to our attention by a simple 3 X 5 card tacked to the bulletin board: "President Kennedy was shot in Dallas this morning." The emotional impact of this news was absorbed in silence, since our next "break day" coincided with JFK's funeral, which we watched on TV along with millions of other Americans.

The counterpoint to these external events was the deep silence of the Spiritual Exercises, in which we were led into an awareness of the sacredness of life and the openness to "finding God in all things." I came to value the interior life, relishing what Gerard Manley Hopkins called "the dearest freshness deep down things."

Over the ensuing eleven years, the external events through which I moved as a Jesuit shaped my sense of who I was in the world. Through the lens of history the Kennedy assassination ushered in a turbulent period in American life—the free speech movement, race riots, the Vietnam War, the assassinations of Robert Kennedy and Martin Luther King, the counter-cultural upheaval of the '60s, Woodstock, Watergate. The small story of my life as a Jesuit played out within the backdrop of these big stories of our time in history. My roles in relationship to this history shifted from passive observation to reaction (joining in Vietnam War protests) to interpretation (leading students to reflect on these events) to change agent (working on

George McGovern's presidential campaign and later through community organizing).

What about the interior life? I found comfort in silence. Prayer and meditation assumed more of a reflection on experience as it unfolded, aided by daily journaling. Without realizing it at the time, I was embracing the unique charism of Ignatius—"contemplation in action." This became a thread woven through my life in the years to come.

A few pivotal experiences and insights stand out as transformative in the time since I left the Society in 1974. The first was my dawning awareness of deep continuity amidst all the changes and upheavals in my life—that I could trust the rhythm of death and rebirth, mourning and new discovery, that are a part of these transitions. My external journey has taken me to Oakland, Bellingham, Reno, Portland, and to an 80-acre forested farm in Oregon's Columbia River Gorge. There have been times of great joy: meeting and marrying the love of my life, Julie Burns; the birth of my sons, Jake and Hank; their high school and college graduations; Hank's marriage to Kerry in 2003 and Jake's marriage to Nancy in 2013. Times of sadness have included the deaths of our parents, deaths of friends and loved ones, mistakes, and unrealized expectations. I have been blessed with a satisfying profession as a psychologist. This year I retired, allowing more time for tending our farm, doing some consulting, volunteering with a non-profit organization Julie and I started a decade ago, and travel.

My time as a community organizer in the public housing projects of Chicago and the rural farms and towns of Northwest Washington taught me how political power functions and how vulnerable and disenfranchised people can gain power to influence their lives and neighborhoods through organized action.

John F. Christensen

The births of my sons gave me a profound sense of my own mortality and my responsibility for others—that I had been given a finite period of time to work with Julie to protect, nurture, and mentor them into the beginning of their journey through life. My relationship with Julie has taught me the deeper meaning of love as a journey, rather than a destination, involving the work of communication and compromise, as well as delight in presence to the one you love. We call our farm "Pilgrims' Pause," since we view life as a pilgrimage, and the forest and land that we steward as a place of rest on our own journey, as well as for other pilgrims who stop here along their way.

The study and practice of "mindfulness" as expressed in the Buddhist traditions has helped me appreciate in a new way the Ignatian notion of detachment. I came gradually to the realization that to embrace the world as it really is—constantly changing—requires letting go continuously of where we have been in order to be present to what is emerging in the next moment. I came to appreciate emotions as weather systems that are passing through, to which I can be fully present without clinging to them or regarding them as defining of me or other people. As such, mindfulness of emotions seemed to me like Ignatius's discussion of the alternation of consolation and desolation.

All of this was brought home to me about twenty years ago while I was making a retreat at the Nestucca Sanctuary on the Oregon coast. I had meditated on the passage from John's Gospel where Jesus, "knowing that he had come from God and was going to God," washed the feet of his disciples in the context of their final meal. Later as I was walking along a forest path I realized that each step was a movement "from God and to God." This became a metaphor for my life as I moved through my days, from one encounter to another, from consolation to desolation to consolation, traveling from place to place, from in-breath to out-breath. This is my understanding of what Ignatius meant by "finding God in all things."

The counterpoint of the interior life and engagement in the external world that moved through my life as a young Jesuit is gradually resolving into the awareness that there is a single experience of life and reflection. Mindfulness in the Buddhist tradition is being a contemplative in action, *simul in actione contemplativus.* This fruit of the Spiritual Exercises, sown over fifty years ago, is the continuous thread woven through my life. It is much like the thread described by William Stafford in the following poem:

The Way It Is

There is a thread you follow. It goes among
things that change. But it doesn't change.
People wonder about what you are pursuing.
You have to explain about the thread.
But it is hard for others to see.
While you hold it you can't get lost.
Tragedies happen; people get hurt
or die; and you suffer and get old.
Nothing you do can stop time's unfolding.
You don't ever let go of the thread.

John Christensen was in the California Province from 1963 to 1974. He and Julie Burns Christensen live at their retreat, "Pilgrims' Pause," in Sandy, Oregon. John holds a PhD in Clinical Psychology, which he practiced for many years, and he now writes and consults on Medical Ethics and Clinical Psychology in Portland, Oregon, and elsewhere.

One Door Closed and Another Opened

Juanita Cordero

During the school year of 1969 I came to the realization that God was calling me from my life as a religious sister to follow another path. A Jesuit brother alerted me to a job opening at St. Francis, a Jesuit parish in Arizona. I flew there for an interview and landed the job teaching first grade. Don Cordero, a newly ordained Jesuit and close friend was assigned to the Kino House in Tucson while studying for his Masters in Counseling. As faith would have it, he would stop by to see me on the way down to Tucson. A few years later we realized we were in love. After telling the pastor of our intent to get married, I was fired from my job, told I was a scandal to the parish, and excommunicated. Don decided then to leave the Jesuits and join me in Arizona. After a year we moved back to California and raised our five children.

I had always felt called to priesthood since childhood but could not answer that call when I was growing up due to canon 1024, which states that only men can be ordained priests.

God had other plans for me, however, as I found out about a group of women who had been ordained on the Danube River in Germany in 2002. I contacted Patricia Fresen, one of the bishops from Germany, and was accepted into the program for Roman Catholic Women Priests. Don was very supportive of my calling, and we even went to Germany and Austria to visit some of the women who had been ordained on the Danube. I was ordained a deacon in Pittsburgh, Pennsylvania, on July 31, the feast of St. Ignatius Loyola, with eleven other women. This was the first such ordination in the United States.

One Door Closed and Another Opened

A year later, on the feast of Mary Magdalen, I was ordained the first woman priest in California at Casa de Maria in Santa Barbara. My first Mass was a celebration of our thirty-six wonderful years of marriage as Don was dying from prostate cancer, and I wanted God to bless those beautiful years of commitment together.

Don was very weak and could not stand at the altar to concelebrate with me, but he gave the most powerful homily I have ever heard. It is one I will always treasure. He was anointed by each member of the Magdala Catholic Community and requested that I preside at his funeral service, which took place on January 5, 2008.

I continue to bring the sacraments to the faithful wherever God calls me. I have presided at baptisms, weddings, first communions, liturgies, anointing of the sick, and funerals. As a woman priest I feel very privileged to serve the homeless, the marginalized, and the sick and dying. As Don would always tell me, "God is a tricky God, and you never know where he will lead you." I thank God each day for that tricky God who calls me, always, to serve others as a woman priest.

Juanita Cordero has, for many years, been a Compañera, first with her Compañero husband Don (California Province 1955–71), and now as a friend to many Jesuits and former Jesuits, and to the poor in the Southwest. She is a leader in the Roman Catholic Women Priests organization.

Choosing to Live a Nonviolent Life

John S. Dear

We need to train ourselves in the methodologies and practice of nonviolence to unleash the holy, holistic power of nonviolence in every part of our individual, interpersonal and global lives. As we do, we will discover, as Dr. King did, a peaceful way to live and deal with the world. "I plan to stand by nonviolence," he said shortly before he died, "because I have found it to be a philosophy of life that regulates not only my dealings in the struggle for racial justice but also my dealings with people and with my own self."

As we take new steps forward in the nonviolent life, we will discover, to our amazement, how to be more peaceful and what it means to be a human being.

I believe we were created to be nonviolent and that the whole human family was designed by the God of peace to live and practice nonviolence. Organized religion, schools and universities, and the world's governments should therefore teach, practice, and pass on the wisdom of nonviolence. Because we have given ourselves over to the forces and systems of violence instead, we have to teach ourselves how to be nonviolent, and get involved personally in creating grassroots movements of nonviolence, if the world is to survive.

More than that, nonviolence is what the spiritual life is all about. God, we are learning, is a God of nonviolence. A Godly life, then, is a nonviolent life. Every one of us is on a journey toward our loving, nonviolent God.

Choosing to Live a Nonviolent Life

John Dear entered the Maryland Province in 1982. His book The Nonviolent Life, *from which this piece is an excerpt that he wanted to share, was published in late 2013 by Pace e Bene Press. Soon after, he was dismissed from the Society of Jesus after living, teaching, and preaching in the Order for almost thirty-two years. He currently works with Pace e Bene Nonviolence Service— Education, Resources and Action for Nonviolent Change—founded in 1989.*

From Jesuit to Married Catholic Worker

Eric C. DeBode

I entered the Jesuits in 1983 at the age of nineteen. I had no idea what I was doing. My faith was important to me, and somehow I felt that by entering the Jesuits I had found a way to make a total offering of myself for the ideals of service that mattered to me. I explored these stirrings within me during the novitiate experiments by working with the homeless and struggling with questions of poverty and social justice.

My journey continued as I studied politics at Santa Clara University and philosophy at Gonzaga. During summers I alternated study programs one year with trips to Mexico and Central America the next. I had encountered the Catholic Worker and spent a lot of time reading Dorothy Day and visiting the Catholic Workers in Los Angeles.

Although I was learning a lot, and experiencing so many new things with my travels, I struggled with lots of questions about my vocation as many of us did. I also fell in love a couple of times which led me to question whether I could remain a Jesuit for life.

Finally, while at Dolores Mission in East Los Angeles for Regency, I called my Provincial to discuss my future. I shared that I looked forward to theology very much, and that after ordination I felt called to work with the homeless, do Central America solidarity work, and perhaps live at a Catholic Worker house. As you might imagine, the Provincial clearly, but delicately, let me know how unlikely that plan was.

I spent a year discerning my options with my spiritual director. I was full of gratitude, and remain so today, for every minute I spent in the Jesuits. I don't regret, in any way, my decision to leave. I knew that my deepest desires were centered more on a Catholic Worker life and spirituality.

My decision to leave turned on the fact that I didn't want to fight the Jesuits so that I could fight for justice. That clarity was a grace that helped me tremendously as I moved forward into the work I wanted to do, and deeper into the spirituality that fed me.

So, after nine years, I left the Jesuits to run a drop-in center for the homeless for a couple of years. Then, I landed back in Los Angeles at the Catholic Worker for about five years. Eventually I met Alice Linsmeier, who worked with Jesuit Refugee Service in El Salvador and Los Angeles. Our life paths mirrored each other; we had scores of friends in common, and we almost met a few times over the previous twenty years. It was a quick and easy choice to marry.

We live in Half Moon Bay at the Catholic Worker with our two children, Liliana (10) and Javier (5). Alice is a farm-worker leadership-team trainer for OxfamUSA with their "Equitable Food Initiative," a project shared by farm-worker unions, National Farmworker Ministries, Pesticide Action Network and others. She trains teams on farms both nationally and internationally. It is a continuation of her efforts on behalf of worker justice. Her local work in Half Moon Bay is for immigration reform and justice for immigrants. Alice's work helps us to pay for our extra family costs.

The Catholic Worker operates a House of Hospitality for homeless families; a free community breakfast program; the "Garden of Eatin'" project where we take homeless folks and unemployed farm-workers to an organic farm to work twice each week; we vigil for Peace on Highway 1 every

Tuesday, and lots more. We are living simply, working with the homeless and struggling poor, and doing peacemaking. I feel pretty happy!

This past summer I helped organize a thirty-year reunion for some members of the Class of 1983. It was lovely to gather with some who stayed in the Jesuits and others who left, and hear the stories of life's twists and turns. It was fascinating to see that we were all pretty much the same; just older, deeper, and more advanced in our "professions." The transitions in our lives seemed less about dramatic changes, and more about becoming our truer selves, and aligning our innermost stirrings with our daily lives. That's a grace to be grateful for indeed.

Eric DeBode (California Province 1983–92) and Alice Linsmeier and family live and work in Half Moon Bay, California

A Jesuit Falls in Love

John F. Devine

The date was January 3, 1966. The place was the John Carroll front parlor in the Healy Building, one of the most solemn sites on the Georgetown University campus. Any passerby peeking through the nineteenth century lace-curtained windows could see Betty and me sitting there facing one another under the twelve-foot ceiling. I had ushered Betty over to this quiet and venerable spot as an attempt to get away from the bustle of the busy office where we both worked. At the time I was known as Father John Devine, SJ, Dean of Students. Betty Duffee had been my secretary since 1964, two years after her divorce.

I really had no idea how she would take the news, so I just came out with it and said: "I have been accepted in the University of Arizona doctoral program in anthropology, and I'll be leaving Georgetown next week." Betty knew of my interest in anthropology but more importantly she knew that I needed to get away and reflect on our relationship and figure out what I was going to do with the rest of my life. For her, there was no torment, no doubt, no angst. And when she got the news, there were no tears, no drama. She looked at me directly in the eyes and just said "John Devine, I love you." Years later, after we had married and when we reflected back on that moment, I used to tease her: how were you ever brave enough to say "John Devine"? How come you didn't use my proper title and say "Father Devine, I love you"? She would just laugh.

For Betty, our relationship was quite simple: if two people loved one another, that was all there was to it. They should express that love in marriage. For my part, conditioned through some twenty years in the Jesuits, it was not so simple: there were many issues to be resolved—my vows of poverty, chastity and obedience, my priesthood, my entire Jesuit identity. Where would I work? How would I support Betty and her children as I had zero resources? So for me the *sturm und drang* continued as I headed out to Tucson, Arizona.

Leaving my job itself as Dean of Students was not a problem for me. Deep down, I hated the position. The entire Jesuit community recognized that it was the most thankless job in the university. Over a beer in the recreation room many of my friends would extend their sympathies. They knew that I had switched from my teaching position in the theology department reluctantly and only because "holy obedience" dictated it.

When I arrived at Tucson everyone could not have been kinder. The University of Arizona was rated as having one of the best anthropology departments in the country. I felt honored to have been accepted. I quickly got to know some of the other graduate students and the department staff. I visited the seventeenth century Jesuit mission of San Xavier del Bac several miles south of Tucson. I was living at the Newman Center where I said Mass each morning. In a word, for a month I tried to adjust to this new lifestyle.

In the evenings I began reading James Joyce's *A Portrait of the Artist as a Young Man*. I found Joyce's experiences with the Jesuits to be remarkably similar to my own. I still felt close enough to the order to remain very attached to it yet part of me was becoming alienated.

Very soon I would have to register and pay the tuition. I knew that at that point I would be committing myself and my Jesuit superior to graduate study on a long-term basis. Feeling more and more alone and depressed, I found myself cast into a decision-making situation for which I was quite ill-prepared. Of course I should have considered all of this while I was still at Georgetown. But all I knew for sure was that I wanted

Betty and I needed her desperately. I could not imagine life without her. I knew I could certainly not face a five-year doctoral program without her.

By the end of January I had resigned from the anthropology program and checked out of all of my commitments in Tucson. Within a few days more I was headed back to Washington. But I could not bear going back to Georgetown. How could I explain to my Jesuit brethren what had transpired? Instead I checked in to the Holiday Inn in Arlington just across the Key Bridge from the university. I contacted my friend Father Angelo D'Agostino, SJ, the psychiatrist who was working at the Medical Center. I asked Dag to contact the Provincial for me.

When Betty got the news, she came running over to the motel from her home in McLean. We collapsed into one another's arms and made love. We both knew I had made the right decision in coming back East but we also knew I had only gotten myself deeper in the woods. I was still very much a Jesuit. I still had the three vows. I was still Father Devine. What would happen to me next? I had never felt so out of control of my life.

I don't know what Father Dag and the Provincial (Father Sponga) talked about. I just know that I was instructed to come over to Baltimore and check myself into Mercy Hospital. I was placed in a psychiatric bed so I assume that the Provincial thought I was having a nervous breakdown. After a day or two I was transferred over to the Jesuit community at Loyola College. At the same time, the Provincial, who was a great believer in psychotherapy, thought it would be a good idea if I began to see Dr. Godenne, a famous psychiatrist over at Johns Hopkins. So I began treatment with her almost immediately. After our first session she indicated that she would be happy to continue seeing me, but on one condition: I had to stop seeing Betty. I told her that I would find that impossible. So that was the end of my therapy with Dr. Godenne.

Now I shall try to collapse the rest of my brief biography into one paragraph (to be expanded later.) I spent the following year (1966–67) at Harvard's anthropology department. By May of '67 I had finally made up my mind; I called Betty from Cambridge and told her of my decision. Yes, it was true: we were going to get married. She was ecstatic; so were all of her five children, the three older ones (Caroline, Carl and Laurie) and the two who were still school-aged (Mark and Jonathan). Betty and I were married on January 27, 1968. Betty died peacefully on June 2, 2011 after 43 years of a blissful married life, first in Evanston, Illinois, then in Greenwich Village, NYC (our NYU years) and finally at Cape May Point, New Jersey. The five children and seven grandchildren (Donnie, Jamie, Christine, Melanie, Stephanie, Arianna, and Gianmarco) have all adopted me, a blessing I appreciate more every day.

Betty never accepted the labels that had been pinned on me when I left the order—"exclaustration" and "laicization"—nor did I. For her I had always remained a Jesuit priest, a priest according to the order of Melchizedek. But we both always recognized that it was in the Healy parlor that the defining moment of our relationship had occurred. Her words did not just describe the reality of our love; they created that love just as at the beginning of the Book of Genesis God said "Let there be light" and there was light. So Betty said "let there be love" and there was love.

John Devine (Maryland Province 1945–67) is an anthropologist and author. After retiring from teaching at NYU, he joined the faculty at the Center for Social and Emotional Education in New York City. He lives at the Cedar Crest retirement community in Pompton Plains, New Jersey.

Four Happy Turning Points

Joseph J. Feeney, SJ

I was a happy baby, my mother once told me, and helped by my family and friends, I became a happy and confident kid in Philadelphia's colonial Germantown. In 1948, I entered St. Joseph's Prep, a great school, which provided my first two turning points.

Junior year brought me a faith crisis as I asked, "Is there a God?" "Is Christ God?" and "Is the Catholic Church the Church of Christ?" I read, prayed, and talked with the Jesuit Student Counselor who gave wise and helpful advice. So did a Jesuit scholastic when I asked in class, "A Catholic friend of mine no longer believes in God—what should he do?" Without missing a beat, the scholastic answered, "He has an obligation under God to leave the Church." Happily, the honesty of this answer, and my talks with the Student Counselor and with God helped me reaffirm my faith with joy and full intellectual integrity.

My second turning point, again at the Prep, was deciding to become a Jesuit. I'd been thinking about being a teacher, a lawyer, or a priest, and deep down I knew I wanted to be a Jesuit priest but couldn't admit it, even to myself. I remember once looking out a bus window on the way home from the Prep and feeling I was on a roller-coaster: "I want to be a Jesuit," "No, I don't," "Yes, I do," "No," "Yes," "Yes," "No . . . " "??" Before graduation, I finally admitted my vocation to myself, told the Student Counselor, told my family and friends, and applied to the Society. I've never looked back, and I've fulfilled two of my three desires: priest and teacher. It's all made me a deeply happy SJ.

Four Happy Turning Points

My two other turning points came to me as a Jesuit, involving my tertianship (a final year of spiritual training) and the Jesuit poet Gerard Manley Hopkins. After studying theology at Woodstock College (1962–66), I hoped to get a PhD in English, and asked to do tertianship with the English Jesuits at St. Beuno's College. My request was granted, and tertianship and my travels gave me an international perspective. The tertians themselves were international—from England, Scotland, Italy, Canada, the United States, Venezuela, Colombia, and Australia—and the director was the storied and lovable Paul Kennedy, SJ. St. Beuno's itself was on a rural hillside in beautiful North Wales near the Irish Sea, and my priestly work brought me to London, St. Helen's, Rhyl, Dublin, and Limerick. Since Europe was so cheap at that time (remember Arthur Frommer's book *Europe on 5 Dollars a Day*?), American Jesuits studying in Europe were told, "Go a month early, stay a month late, and travel: it'll benefit whatever you do later." The first summer a Jesuit friend and I went from Paris to Munich, Vienna, Zurich, and back. Then I crossed the Channel and toured England and Scotland with a fellow tertian. The next summer brought me to Amsterdam, Cologne, Trier, and cities in Italy and Spain including Venice, Florence, and Rome. All this was a turning point in my life, making me see and think internationally. It also prepared me well for grad studies at the University of Pennsylvania (1967–71) and a life of teaching at Saint Joseph's University, with visiting professorships at Georgetown, Santa Clara, and Seattle Universities.

My fourth turning point came in England in the summer of 1977 when, by chance, I saw a note on the bulletin board at the Jesuits' Campion Hall in Oxford about a celebration at St. Beuno's later that summer for the centennial of Gerard Manley

Hopkins' ordination there. I had done no work in Hopkins at Penn, but I thought the U.S. should also celebrate his ordination, so when I got home I read everything Hopkins wrote about priesthood and wrote an article for *America* magazine—it became the cover article for the December 3, 1977, issue: "Nature's Round Makes Jubilee: Hopkins's Priestly Centenary." This was the first article I ever wrote about Hopkins and provided my fourth turning point: I became a Hopkins scholar, later co-editing *The Hopkins Quarterly* (1994–present) and a book of essays on Hopkins (2002), writing *The Playfulness of Gerard Manley Hopkins* (2008), recording a box of CDs/DVDs entitled *Gerard Manley Hopkins: Magician of Words, Sounds, Images, and Insights* (2013), publishing eighty Hopkins articles and giving eighty-six Hopkins lectures in Europe, Asia, and America. In 1998 I even discovered in London an unknown poem of his, "'Consule Jones,'" and published it in *TLS, The Times Literary Supplement*.

Such were the four turning points of my life, coming in many places and forms and changing my life. God's ways are strange indeed, but these pivotal events have made me, at seventy-nine, a blessed, happy, and grateful Jesuit. Amen, amen.

Joe Feeney, SJ, entered the Maryland Province in 1952. He teaches at Saint Joseph's University, Philadelphia, and continues to do scholarly work associated with Gerard Manley Hopkins, SJ.

My 50th Anniversary as a Jesuit Priest
October 22, 2013

Paul Fitterer, SJ

All of us are on a journey. My fellow jubilarians and each of you present, and all of us, whatever our circumstances, have responded to a call—a personal call, unique to each; all of us have a vocation from God. Believing that, thirteen years ago, in the year 2000, when I celebrated fifty years as a Jesuit, I asked the question "would I respond to that call again? Would I do it again?"

This is no light or easy question. To it then I answered "I'm not sure." I said this before Seattle Prep students, many friends and family gathered for the Jubilee celebration of my fifty years of my being in the Jesuits. And as you can imagine, many were surprised at the answer. But it was true: I did not know. Those were troubled times in the Oregon Province of the Society of Jesus: clergy abuse, bankruptcy, hierarchical cover up, diminished respect for what once was considered a noble calling.

So if I answered then, "I'm not sure", it is still a fair question now. To address the question, I saw that now my answers to the deeper questions that I then asked were almost the same as they were thirteen year ago—I am filled with such gratitude, blessed by education and training, shaped by a spirituality, theology and psychology—which has allowed me to deal with, live into the mystery of the Life in whom we live. I have been provided a holistic framework of meaning that holds together, that holds me together.

I have a simple rule that allows me to judge the success or failure of my life. Am I more open? Open to God, open to truth, open to responsibility, open to people? I judge this openness by these considerations:

- I know, ever more deeply, that Freedom and centered love not guilt and fear are the results of healthy religion.
- I have learned with much wrestling that there can be no contradiction between science, religion, spirituality, psychology. If there seems to be it's because we don't know enough about one or the other.
- I believe the Church is a community of the Body of Christ—whose voice must be respected in a Catholic's decision making. However no one can take away the freedom of my conscience—neither Pope, Church, or State, and freedom is not license to do what you want but power to do what you ought.
- I believe the Church is primarily the People of God, not primarily a hierarchical structure issuing fiats. And there are two important constituents of the people of God:
  - our lay companions, men and women, have done so much to shape the Jesuit enterprise in the Northwest universities, high schools, parishes. This is particularly true as I reflect on lay women's and religious women's friendship in my life. I am grateful to them.

- - The other group—our young people in our high schools and universities and parishes, and this service will continue among us: The young people are the future of the Church and the world!
- One more remark about women: the Martha/Mary story has so many levels of meaning—among which is an invitation to openness to women's ordination. "She sat at the feet of the Lord to hear his word." In the tradition of Israel "sitting at the feet of the Master" was only for males, rabbis in training. Not so for Jesus. Jesus respected the leadership of women.
- And finally, prayer. In Ignatian terms, prayer is an opening to the immediate experience of God. For over twenty years I have directed ordained Jesuits, Novices, laypeople, religious women in the Spiritual Exercises of St Ignatius in thirty-day and other retreats—I have seen God work. As Carl Jung said: "I don't believe in God. I know God."

These things I say now with even deeper conviction—rooted in my Catholic tradition and shaped by my Jesuit heritage. So is this enough to give an answer. Well, I would continue the answer as I did in 2000: I have been blessed with so many friends, have been privileged to have a significant impact on people's lives, have been invited and welcomed into intimate family and personal moments. I know of few people who have had this kind of experience, who can continue to strive to find ways to reach out to the poor and marginalized . . . and, most significantly, to experience in all encounters a God who speaks and moves in peoples' lives.

Now to address this question, "Would I do it again:" **I now say, as I did not thirteen years ago, "Yes, I would."** Yes, I would! And were I to say, what has changed that brings me to this? I would have to say, "I'm not sure." Certainly a lot, much that is troubling, remains. But to have a Pope like Francis has been a help. And some things in the gospels continue to inspire me: I, like Mary, have been able to sit at the feet of the Lord, and I have heard his word and have recognized it as "the better part." I, like the battered man the Samaritan encountered on the road, have experienced care and compassion. I experience the challenge of "being neighbor" that Jesus invites me to. I know of no vocation that could allow me to live as well into the invitation of the Good Samaritan story ("Do this and you shall live") or the Martha/Mary story (She sat at the feet of the Lord to hear his word). As I grow older, it seems to me that there are no ideals more important for me to grow into. That's the invitation. Hopefully, in my next fifty years as priest I will hear Jesus clearly and follow Jesus closely, responding to Him who invites and says: "Go and do likewise."

God "knows well," says the prophet Jeremiah, "the plans I have for you."

Paul Fitterer, SJ, has served in the Oregon Province since 1950, providing spiritual direction and support for young Jesuits, and he has for many years taught religion at Gonzaga Preparatory School in Spokane, Washington, and at Seattle Preparatory School, in its Matteo Ricci Program, and often in Seattle University's Masters of Religious Education Program, SUMORE.

The Tree of Life is Green

Donald J. Foran

At some point in my years in the Jesuits, perhaps it was when I taught Literature at Gonzaga Prep in Spokane and the assassinations of Martin Luther King Jr. and Bobby Kennedy took place (1968), perhaps slightly later than that during doctoral studies at USC when I was almost completely on my own, or perhaps it was in the summer of 1973 when I went to jail with the *campesinos* for two weeks in Fresno (an act of civil disobedience to protest workers' being sprayed with insecticides in the fields), I refused to let religion step into the place of life.

Many lines from Literature ("Theory is forever grey, but the tree of life is green" from Goethe, "Time coughs when we would kiss" from Auden, and "for lack of time and thinking, people have to love one another without knowing much about it" from Camus) began to erode what I thought of as my faith. I now have, I believe, a more mature concept of faith, which is more or less contiguous with love for individuals and for humanity as a whole.

Theology, even well-formulated ideas from fine thinkers like Rahner, Segundo, and Schillebeeckx, failed, ultimately, to delight me. Even their imaginative reflections seemed to pale beside the fiction of Melville, Faulkner, Morrison, and Carver and the poetry of Yeats, Hopkins, Heaney, Kunitz, and Oliver. The taunting words of Wallace Stevens's narrator in "High-toned Old Christian Woman" ("Poetry is the Supreme Fiction, Madame") resonated with me, and, over about forty years, I edged away from the Church and the Jesuits, though for some of that time I went through the motions, probably hoping that certain New Testament parables which had always meant a lot to me (The Good Samaritan, The Prodigal Son, The Man Born Blind) had some basis in fact, were not merely "made up" by the Sacred Writers. [I'm now more comfortable with the fact that even if they were made up, such fictions seem to embody what Jesus Christ was all about to his contemporaries and the rest of us.]

I left the Jesuits and the priesthood in 1978 after going through 7000 rads of cobalt for Hodgkin's Disease and spending a time in Kenya studying and reporting on Infant Formula Abuse. I would not meet my wife Maggie until October 1981, so, apart from relationships with my family and a few close friends, I knew tragically little about love in all its wondrous complexity. We married in 1982 and her love for me and mine for her, and the birth of our daughters Amanda and Erin, pretty much blew my mind. I now knew the difference between theory and the "dearest freshness deep down things," which the poet Hopkins intuited and thankfully wrote about in "God's Grandeur."

I began to suspect that Tillich was probably right when he suggested that God is "the ground of our being" or the poet Dylan Thomas proclaimed in "The Force That Through the Green Fuse Drives the Flower," which drives my green age and that of all who are driven. In other words, I had shifted from a religion-centered idea of faith to a nature-centered concept that might, ultimately, be—who can grasp this and appreciate this?—religious.

I'm grateful for the religio-theological teachers and institutions that have helped me go somewhat beyond what I once embraced, or, more realistically perhaps, walk along beside. My excitement for life is now not exactly pantheistic and I do not consider it at all atheistic. I believe that my quixotic forays into the unknown and what can perhaps be known are, well, agnostic and thus, possibly, humanistic and, thus, unexpectedly, astoundingly, sacred.

Don Foran entered the novitiate at Sheridan, Oregon, in 1961 and left the Society and the priesthood in November 1978. He earned his PhD in English at USC in Los Angeles and a post-doc MA in theology from JSTB in Berkeley. He recently retired from forty-four years of teaching, mostly Literature and Writing. He and his wife Maggie live in Olympia, Washington. His literary, spiritual, and social-justice interests are unfurled at http://donforan.webs.com.

Vocation Discernment

John Fuchs, SJ

In the process of sorting through my cardboard boxes of notes, letters, photos, articles and other nostalgia which I had hauled around with me since high school, I came across this essay I wrote approximately twenty-one years ago, an account of a religious experience I had forty-three years ago!

I decided to preserve this one relic since I thought it might be helpful to others. What I wrote then is no less true to me today.

I first entered the Society of Jesus in 1960, right out of high school. Then I left the Society nine years later, after my second-year regency, which was one of the most difficult decisions I have ever had to make. Although I have never regretted my decision to leave, I ended up re-entering the Society three years later, after much discernment. Since re-entering the Society of Jesus, I have never had any regrets or second thoughts. I am only grateful for God's patience and fidelity. Here is the account of the experience I re-discovered:

There was once a time when I thought I would never know what I wanted in life or what God wanted for me. Since then I have discovered that being a Jesuit and a priest is not what I want most. Being a Jesuit priest is a precious gift and one I am continually grateful for, but it is not what is most important to me. This sounds less than edifying even as I say it, but I know this to be true.

Perhaps I would have never known this had I not left the Society and returned. Through this unusual experience God taught me that, far more important than being a Jesuit, or anything else for that matter, was my willingness to surrender myself totally and allow God's providential love to govern my life. This self-emptying and allowing God's Holy Spirit to sustain and guide me on my journey, especially without my needing to know the destination, is what I treasure most and what I will always be most grateful for. For me this conversion experience of becoming more like Jesus in humility and docility to the Holy Spirit is the treasure hidden in the field or the pearl of great price for which I am willing to sell everything.

*This grace of offering myself to God without reservation resulted mysteriously in my being called back to the Society, but I was genuinely willing to accept wherever I was being led. Because I had finally found the way, I could be more indifferent to my destination and, ironically, more free to know what I really wanted. For that brief moment in the chapel at Sheridan it felt like I had courageously leapt from the Second Class to the Third Class of Persons and perhaps for the first time in my life I found myself resting in God's unconditional love. My unconditional surrender opened me to receiving more intimately God's unconditional surrender to me (*Suscipe*) so that my vocation in life could be not merely mine, nor God's, but ours. The additional gift of being called back to the Society and the priesthood seemed to flow spontaneously from this primary gift of intimacy with God, for with this I was truly rich enough and needed nothing more. From this point on my vocation discernment seemed relatively easy and almost embarrassingly obvious.*

Now I am spending the rest of my life trying to understand and relish, even as I write this, that crucial religious experience of twenty-two years ago, for it is the foundation of my life today. I keep reminding myself that I do not need to be a Jesuit priest, but I find myself wanting to be. God does not need me to be, but He wants this for me. It is what we want together.

Why do I want to be a Jesuit priest and why do I continue to choose to be? I am tempted to say it is because I want to freely give what I have freely received, or because I want to help others, especially those most in need, or because of the companionship of my brother Jesuits. But as good and noble as these reasons may be they are, by themselves, inadequate, and, at least for me, ultimately unconvincing (Third Time of Election). My Jesuit vocation seems more like a "consolation without previous cause" for which I can find no satisfactory explanation. For there are many times I simply do not like apostolic work or priestly and sacramental ministry, living community and celibate life, being accountable to superiors, and whatever else makes up my life as a Jesuit. My disliking, which at times can be rather intense, occasionally scandalizes me, leaving me to wonder if in fact I have made the wrong choice, even after such a long, painful, thorough, and dramatically clear discernment.

But what continues to save me from this potentially endless cycle of self-doubt and almost ludicrous denial of God's grace is for me to keep remembering the freedom and consolation out of which my election originated. Whatever desolation I may experience at any given time, regardless of its cause or persuasion, not only does not invalidate my call but by sheer contrast makes it clear just how radically gratuitous and irrevocable this call really is. It is true that "The devil knows not for whom he works," for eventually this desolation ends up helping confirm my call!

What a relief to know that his vocation is not simply my idea or desire, but God's in me. In fact this is what we pray at our first vows, "As you have freely given me the desire to make this offering, so also give me the abundant grace to fulfill it." In allowing God to continue to choose this life in me, God, who fortunately knows me far better than I know myself, will help me fulfill my most intimate, unconscious desires and reveal to me my truest identity.

John Fuchs, SJ, entered the Oregon Province in 1960, left in 1969, and then entered again in 1972. He is superior of the Jesuit community at Bellarmine Prep in Tacoma, Washington and is sought out as a spiritual director and retreat director by many in the Northwest and beyond.

The First Night

(upon retirement, written during an 8-day retreat in Sedalia, Colorado, August 2013)

James T. Gilroy

Lightning struck and shattered
the night's north wind,
unsettling the thoughts and moods
of words harmonized on the back
of a cricket
droning deeper and spinning
fits of uncommon sleep.
Yet the subtle peace of place,
the worn wood and hand-worked stone,
a bosom soft with open lace and warmth,
stirred an appetite,
a being
hungry for what might be divine in this
restless night.

Jim Gilroy entered the California Province in 1964 and left ten years later. He was an educator for over thirty years. He and his wife, Mary, live in San Cristobal, New Mexico.

Movement to New Possibilities

Peter J. Henriot, SJ

Most of my life has been devoted to "development, justice and peace." Even before joining the Oregon Province Jesuits in 1956, I was preparing to become President of the USA as an undergraduate at Santa Clara University. Well, the Jesuits distracted me from that political campaign! But in spirituality, training and experience the Jesuits gave me the foundation for a committed and competent involvement in issues of development, justice and peace.

Ignatian spirituality opened me to seeing God in the riches and the poverty of our everyday world. Studies at University of Chicago and Harvard trained me to do the analysis necessary to understand the structural challenges and processes of changing social situations. And experience of injustices in racial relations, poverty situations, treatment of women, and environmental crises moved my heart as much as my mind.

So my social and political work from 1971 to 1988 was at the Center of Concern in Washington DC—research, education and advocacy on national and international issues concerning those key issues. I was living in a small Jesuit insertion community in an African-American neighborhood in DC where we shared simple lifestyle and prayerful engagement, and, during one of those years, for tertianship, I lived in a barrio in Medellin, Colombia.

Then in 1989 I left Washington, DC for Lusaka, Zambia, working at the Jesuit Centre for Theological Reflection until 2011. More research, education and advocacy on the African realities of development, justice and peace. (One of those years

I spent in a village program in southern Zambia.) I grew in understanding and passion about the consequences of colonialism, past and present, as a member of the young and vibrant Zambia-Malawi Province.

Always enriching and shaping this work was the pastoral experience of serving in a parish. On Capitol Hill in DC and in a poor neighborhood in Washington, and then in a poor rural community outside Lusaka. Experiencing people's real lives in ordinary experiences moved my thoughts and emotions in this social and political work in a more "radical" direction. I was arrested in Washington DC demonstrations, denounced in newspapers in Lusaka, but always supported and strengthened, challenged and confronted, by my brothers in the Jesuit communities in which I've been privileged to share life.

Books and articles written, classes and seminars taught, presentations and consultations with a wide variety of audiences: always the development, justice and peace themes predominated!

A powerful influence, of course, was—and still is—the explicit expression of my Jesuit mission as formulated by General Congregation 32: "the service of faith and the promotion of justice" as integrally and necessarily united. Father Pedro Arrupe was my mentor and inspiration. My participation in General Congregation 33 meant a chance to help make that mission of faith and justice even more clear and prominent.

So how do I explain now the "transition" that has taken hold of me in recent years? Out of the political sphere, away from the socio-economic involvements, down from the public engagements? For the past three years I've been fund-raiser (that's definitely not FUN-raiser!) for a new Jesuit secondary school in Malawi.

How can the present work for fundraising for a school be related to previous involvement in development, justice and peace? Is this not a very "disjointed transition"? That question comes often to me, from my friends and especially from myself.

Well, what is this school I'm raising funds for? When we began talking about such a project several years ago, many people in Malawi said, "Oh, you Jesuits—you will start up a private boys school in the capital, Lilongwe." Yes, very exclusive, very expensive, very "special." Well, it is indeed "special"—as a real "option for the poor."

The new high school is not in the capital, but in a poor rural area 75 miles outside the capital—an area where less than 25% of the youth (less than 20% of the girls) go to secondary school. It is not an all-boys school, but a co-educational school from the start, aiming for gender equity. There is boarding for everyone (500-plus of Grades Nine to Twelve). And not a private school but one that cooperates with the Government of Malawi, which pays the teachers. That means fees are less than 400 US dollars a year—making the school more accessible to families of lesser means.

Loyola Jesuit Secondary School (LJSS) will open for Grade Nine in September 2014 and will continue to grow—if the fundraiser does his job! It exists in one of the poorest countries in the world (170 out of 187 on the UN Human Development Index). But Malawi is a peaceful country with democratic traditions, thank God! Yet a country with no real future possible unless Malawian youth are educated!

So, I do experience that I'm still in "development justice and peace" ministry! In a transition to a new mission that promotes development through education, assures justice through gender equity, and instills peace through the values of Ignatian pedagogy.

Exciting—yes! Enriching—yes! Challenging—yes, for sure, especially since I write this as I approach my 78th birthday. I've been told that Jesuits get "tired" but never get "retired." Well, that's what my transition is all about, thank God!

10 April, 2014 Lilongwe, Malawi

Peter Henriot, SJ, (Oregon Province 1956, Zambia-Malawi Province 1992) invites inquiry about Loyola Jesuit Secondary School in Malawi and his efforts to support that mission. Go to http://www.loyola-malawi.org. His e-mail is phenriot14@gmail.com.

Passing Brothers

Rodney P. Herold

Jim and I shared the past seventy-one-plus years on Earth. I have often considered us as "twins," just born ten years apart. The one picture that caught my attention as I flipped through our family album for his memorial the day before Thanksgiving was a snapshot of us taken looking out over the Willamette Valley.

Our paths were amazingly similar. Our temperaments took after our Dad, who was a civil engineer, and we both loved working with our hands, tinkering with mechanical things. We both went on to teach math and science at the secondary and technical school level. We were both Jesuits for eighteen years

Our paths were different at some points. Jim finished his theology at Alma, was approved for ordination, and then struggled for almost five years trying to find a place for himself in the Jesuits; he never was able to realize his dream as a "perpetual scholastic." He left around 1970 and spent the rest of his life in San Francisco. He always treasured the Jesuits, however; he kept a deck of '64 and '65 ordination cards of his classmates.

I completed my theology in 1973 and was ordained in Seattle in December just after I began community organizing with the Baumann/Helfrich team in Oakland. After two years in Oakland, I moved on to Seattle to organize there. In 1978 I left the Jesuits, primarily frustrated that the Church and the Jesuits were making no headway towards including women among their ranks.

Jim and I were both fiercely independent. Jesuit training had given us both strong educational backgrounds that we were able to utilize. Jim's path after the Jesuits was as a teacher and an entrepreneur.

During the forty years after leaving the Jesuits he bought and ran, solo, three successive small businesses while living in a cottage in the Outer Richmond District of San Francisco.

Since 1978 I have been just as independent. At first, I used my mechanical skills to support myself as a "handyman." To these I added multimedia skills I had developed as an organizer in Oakland and Seattle. I have spent the rest of my life in search of a sustaining community, and I am still looking.

The three oldest of the Herold first cousins, born within two years of each other, have now all passed. Late February 2012 was fateful as our cousin Bill succumbed to dementia, and my brother Jim had a small fire in his kitchen, which, in many ways, marked the beginning of his decline as well.

During 2011, I had spent very good months with Jim at his newly acquired cabin near the Russian River, and only now do I recognize that his difficulty in making decisions at that time was an early sign of his dementia. By April 2013 we were no longer denying the severity of what Jim was facing, and I worked feverishly in May to get a support team in place so he could remain in his house. Four months lapsed, and in September we got the reports from his neuropsychic evaluation. This was the first time I'd heard the term Lewy Body Dementia. Curious to the end, he desperately wanted to know what was happening inside his brain. When I read him the prognosis of Lewy Body, he knew and accepted the inevitable. From the time Crystal, my daughter, visited Jim at the beginning of August 2013 until her final visit less than two months later, the "Old Jim" had faded and Lewy Body had settled in. It became clear that we needed more help. By mid-September Jim moved into assisted living at Vintage Golden Gate, which turned into a nightmare for both of us. At the end of September another cousin, Bob, died.

October got worse, not just because of Jim's health. From my perspective, and from Jim's too, no professional even tried to connect with his spirit. He was still fighting for understanding and was "scared to death." He still struggled with his faith. The "Old Jim" we had known and loved so much was no longer active; the "New Jim" was amazing—fighting, struggling, doing everything he could to connect with people. Few among the staff or residents at Vintage were able to connect with him, but he and I were able to remain connected to the end.

I reached out to Jesuits in San Francisco. Several responded from a posting to the Compañeros announcements venue. He was encouraged. Perhaps the Jesuit that Jim and I both valued most was Dave Clarke. Dave entered a year after Jim; our parents and I got to know him at Sheridan and the Mount. Dave was responsible for my going to Weston for philosophy, and I have many fond memories of him there as well as of his visits through San Francisco when I was at JSTB. During Jim's last weeks I was able to reach Dave at Bea House, and even despite his failing memory I was able to spark some fond memories in him. I had hoped to be able to put the two in touch over the phone, but there weren't enough brain cells firing between them to make that happen. I did speak with Dave after Jim passed and he was very grateful for the update.

Perhaps Jim's greatest blessing in his final two months was the appearance of an angel caretaker, Abby Mayen, who took to him as a daughter might. She left her employment with Vintage and followed him to AgeSong when he moved there the day before Halloween. There came a point in mid-October when Jim couldn't find the words to say what he wanted and he began spelling the words he could not pronounce. I believe that Abby taught him one of the last things he ever learned—her name: "A" "b" "b" "y." On Halloween

Abby got a great picture of him in a witch's hat, delightful mischief in his eyes. He was ready to die but doctors were still saying he could live for six months more; hospice was not yet an option. But AgeSong was a huge improvement.

The past year has been a true blessing for me and amazing in so many ways. People surrounding us were constantly amazed; they had rarely seen such brotherly love. I never thought too much about it; continuing to love just seemed the "right " thing to do. From my perspective the "Old Jim" was not trashed; he simply has recycled!

The biggest misunderstanding I ever had with Jim was once when I asked him for a loan to pay for a down payment on a house, not at all a sure bet in our family. My heart swelled with affection as I heard him say: "The most important thing for me is You." It was only a matter of seconds before I realized that I had misunderstood him; what he had actually said was: "The most important thing for me is the view."

I know Jim would have appreciated the pine casket I found on Vashon Island to acknowledge his Northwest roots. As I stood at the foot of his grave looking down into the concrete vault, I knew I did not need to claim another tree for my own casket; I'd be happy in my brother's vault in an urn with the "view" of his wooden casket.

Jim and Rodney Herold were both in the Oregon Province, 1952–70 and 1960–78. Jim's wife, Dorothy Rossoni, died in 1997. and Jim met his next life-long companion, Ruth McHale, at a Kaiser grieving group. Her grandchildren just began calling Jim "Grandpa" a few months ago.

Rodney is now divorced from Barbara Oswald; they met when she was a Jesuit Volunteer. They have a loving daughter, Crystal, married to Tony Toyama. Barbara and Rodney remain friends and partners and now are both living on the property they bought twenty-seven years ago.

Celebrating 52 Years As a Jesuit

Patrick J. Howell, SJ

I entered the Jesuits at Sheridan, Oregon, the novitiate for Jesuits in the Northwest. I had just finished my BS degree in mathematics at Gonzaga, so the two years of prayer, hiking, handball, pruning apple trees, conversation, and introduction to Jesuit life were an idyllic time for me. I was grateful that I had known so many Jesuits at Gonzaga so that I had a more relaxed, alternative view of the Society.

I was only twenty-one, but my peers, most of whom had entered directly from a Jesuit high school, such as Seattle Prep or Bellarmine Prep in Tacoma, considered me one of the "old men." In the summer of 1962 Fr. Frank Mueller, our novice-master, had us study and present talks on the forthcoming Second Vatican Council. I like to tell the story that when we took a survey of the novices on some key issues for the Council: 75% of them thought that Latin should be retained for celebrating Mass. With my sketchy background in Latin, I was not among the majority. In recent years I have frequently taught courses on the theology of Vatican II, and Pope Francis has given a whole new shot in the arm to advance all the implications of the Council.

The years pass swiftly, but they have been full of grace and certainly much more joy than sorrow.

I was blessed with first-class opportunities for advanced education. After initial studies in spirituality, prayer, Jesuit tradition and a dose of Latin and Greek, I studied philosophy and English literature at Boston College.

Then came three years of high-school teaching at Jesuit High in Portland. I survived the trials and testing by high-school boys and grew to love the personal interaction and challenge of teaching English, creative writing and poetry and advising the high-school newspaper.

This "formation" period of teaching in high school probably accounts for why most Jesuits are such good teachers and homilists. Survival demands that you develop rhetorical skills and a flair for the dramatic—even if it's not native to your personality—in order to grab the attention of twenty-eight sophomore boys for fifty minutes each day.

At the next stage of Jesuit formation, I went to Rome to study at the Gregorian University, one of the most renowned Jesuit universities in the world. *Grazia a Dio*, classes were in Italian, not Latin. It may have been "renowned," but the pedagogy was straight out of the 16th century—mostly lectures to 250 students, many of whom absented themselves.

Of course, besides theology and pastoral formation, Rome was a jumping-off place for other educational opportunities: studying French in Paris and Besançon, visiting the ecumenical, monastic center of Taizé, France, where thousands of young people gather each summer for prayer and faith-sharing, an Easter trip to the Holy Land, making a pilgrimage to the home of Ignatius of Loyola in Basque Country, and, most important, exploring the history, culture, and language of Italy itself. And I had a few personal encounters with Paul VI, who was pope in those years. What a rich opportunity and education!

Finally, after eleven years of preparation, I was ordained in my hometown in Lisbon, North Dakota—the first Catholic priest to be ordained in that little town of 2,000. Worth another story in itself.

Not surprisingly, my ministry has centered on education: high school for thirteen years, and then, after completing a doctorate in ministry at Catholic University in Washington, DC in 1985, the past twenty-eight years at Seattle University involved with the ecumenical development of the School of Theology and Ministry.

But another significant portion of my life has been spiritual care of those who have suffered severe mental illness.

All this arose as a surprise, when I suffered a psychotic breakdown myself at age thirty-five and then recovered through excellent psychiatric care and the good graces and support of family and friends. I recounted my experiences in my first book *Reducing the Storm to a Whisper: The Story of a Breakdown* (Sheed & Ward, 1985). This "grace" led to an amazingly rich ministry with people with mental illness and their families.

Years ago, Fr. Michael J. Buckley, SJ, in an address to Jesuit seminarians, asked, "Is this man sufficiently weak to be a priest?" Is this man weak enough, Buckley asked, "so that he cannot ward off significant suffering from his life, so that he lives with a certain amount of failure, so that he feels what it is to be an average man? Is there any history of confusion, of self-doubt, of interior anguish? Has he had to deal with fear, come to terms with frustrations, or accept deflated expectations?"

These are critical questions, Buckley affirmed, because they probe for weakness.

Why weakness? Because, according to the Epistle to the Hebrews, it is in this deficiency, in this interior lack, in this weakness, that the efficacy of the ministry and priesthood of Christ lies. "For because he himself has suffered and been tempted, he is able to help those who are tempted" (Hebrews 2:18).

I think, after fifty-two years, I can rejoice in being "weak enough" to allow the grace of Christ to shine through and carry the load.

Fr. Patrick Howell, SJ, (Oregon Province 1961) is professor of pastoral theology at Seattle University. A version of this story appeared in The Seattle Times *(September 2, 2011)—one of Pat Howell's regular religion columns, which since 2005 have appeared ten times a year.*

Letter from McLeodganj, Himachal Pradesh
April 7, 2014

Kenneth Ireland

One Sunday this past February, Ashish and I went to the English Mass at the Basilica of Bom Jesu in Goa. Initially we were steered into the line to pass by the shrine of Saint Francis Xavier, which is no more than just a small Baroque-style side altar with his body encased in glass—during Mass people venerating the saint wind through the courtyard of the Jesuit residence.

Once we negotiated our way into the back pew of the church, and began to feel at home with the "Jesuit-ness" of the ceremony, I was able to pay more attention. The priest's sermon was not entirely easy to follow. As he struggled to connect Xavier's religious enthusiasm to martyrdom, something I felt didn't match the facts of his remarkable life nor the current situation of Christians in India, I looked around at the rest of the congregation, mostly Indians—Goans I suspect—and certainly, as English speakers, educated. They were also, as far as I could tell, remarkably uninspired, not unlike the Irish-American parish of my childhood.

The sermon and the ceremony were also disconnected from what was happening at the side altar. Men, women, and children, Christians, Muslims, and Sikhs, pushed their way forward towards the barely visible body of the saint. Ash and I had seen almost identical scenes at the many temples, mosques, shrines, and gurdwaras we've visited across India. What they were seeking was a personal matter—blessing for a new marriage, healing, relief from suffering, forgiveness for a personal transgression, a prayer for a child's good fortune, or perhaps even a superstitious belief that contact with a realized being would produce a child. And to be honest, it also seemed unconnected to the Francis I knew as a Catholic, Jesuit saint. But it was real.

I turned my attention back to the priest at the altar and felt deep compassion, even kinship. He was obviously competent, educated, thoughtful, even a devout, spiritual man who was sincerely trying to connect our messy lives with another dimension. With any luck, I might have turned out like him. In that same moment, I also realized why I'd left the Society.

After I graduated from Dartmouth in 1966, I entered the Jesuits at Shadowbrook—over the objections of my parents—and stayed for more than a decade. When time came for me to be ordained, I took a leave of absence and extended it for two years before I signed my exit papers. I realized that I had to confront, and deal with coming out as a gay man, my addictive personality, and, at the time, it seemed that the most effective path was psychological work rather than prayer or meditation.

I had of course done the spiritual exercises of Father Ignatius many times. The experience was rich. When I was trying to decide whether to leave or stick it out, I undertook them again, as well as trying to recreate some of that experience through a study of the enneagram and beginning Buddhist meditation practice. Then for more than three decades, I either wore the designation "ex-Jesuit" as a badge of honor, or disavowed any value in my religious training except on the rare occasion when I ran into someone from that era.

Twenty-five years ago a chance meeting with a Zen priest who was starting a hospice for people with AIDS turned my attention back to meditation practice. It also allowed me to carefully trace the roots of suffering through a spiritual practice that is agnostic with regard to any particular religious system of beliefs.

Today my experience in the Society grows dim, like a series of events in a very ancient land, but what also remains is a sense of intimacy that feels indelible and timeless. I regard things "spiritual" as reflecting on some of the questions that life presents squarely. Most of the puzzlers of my youth—the struggle of coming out in an unaccepting culture, finding a spiritual expression that suited me, etc.— have faded into the background. I no longer seek the kind of answers that I demanded years ago, though I value seeing things through to the end, even things that do not turn out well.

In my view most of the ordinary language of "spiritual" conversation is inadequate. Describing my particular path as a series of "transitions" feels melodramatic. Speaking of a path or a journey sounds like I just bought some nifty running shoes to train for a marathon at my unlikely age. It feels more like just growing up, looking around and realizing that our lives amount to only a brief second, but in that time we can leave things better than we found them, and realize that we are not alone, and that the universe is vast and awe-inspiring.

Letter from McLeodganj, Himachal Pradesh

Ken Ireland entered the New England Province in 1966 and left almost ten years later. He maintains the Buddha, S.J. blog at http://jesuskoan.blogspot.com. He describes himself there: "I am Ivy League and Jesuit educated (and former Jesuit), a writer/editor, a totally out gay activist, a non-churchy but very focused meditation practitioner—and I hope a good partner, son, brother, and friend." He and his partner, Ashish Gupta, have been spending about half a year volunteering, teaching English to Tibetan refugees and doing Buddhist studies in the Gelupa tradition in McLeodganj, northern India, where the Dalai Lama has established his government in exile.

Losing Faith

Michael R. Johnson

"The new pope, Francis," my Jewish painter friend asked, "a Jesuit, right? Weren't you a Jesuit?" I nodded, "Yeah." "So, what happened?" Allan asked as his existential angst settled in. "Did you lose your faith?" His word "faith" packed a punch. He knew what it was like to be lost. I also knew that I had lost something forty years ago. What exactly was it?

I had been working on my personal memoir and was attempting to write about my ten-year experience as a Jesuit when Allan questioned me. He wasn't the first to ask me about my Jesuit past. For some reason, my having been a Jesuit sparked curiosity. I began writing about the Jesuit experience by starting with its last phase. I was just finishing my three year involvement as a community organizer in Chicago. I could see the neighborhood, the building, the El train tracks, the bedroom, the window, the alley, myself. I was naked staring from the bedroom window down into the alley below, trash was swirling as the El train rumbled along its track so close to our living quarters that I dreamed it was running over me during the fitful sleep of those nights.

We were a group of Jesuit grassroots community organizers living in an abandoned convent in the Pilsen—18th and Paulina. As I pondered the swirl of the alleyway, I felt that everything was good, calm, soothing. I also knew that I was in a state of dissolution. I felt like the alley looked, very empty. I had lost myself in the swirl of activity and loose morals that seemed to be inherent in the nature of grassroots community organizing at that time.

Losing Faith

Had I lost my faith? And, if I had, why did everything seem so calm and peaceful in my confusion and dissolution? In her beauty, my fellow organizer, a Latina, slept calmly on the bed without a twinge of guilt—comfortable in her body.

In contrast to that opening scene of my memoir, Ellen, my wife and confidante for the last forty years, had put an old black and white photo on the refrigerator—a reminder of a time past ("he's so cute"). I was standing in my long black cassock and white Roman collar in front of the Sacred Heart Novitiate, my arms folded, a determined, confident look on my face. I was probably in my third year of Jesuit training. On their monthly family visits, my younger brothers would kid me relentlessly about having to wear a dress. My mother was pissed about how the rector seemed to be taking over my life, and my dad was highly skeptical about living my life "without sex." "How 'bout celibacy, Mike?" Allan was relentless in his query.

"Oh, man that was a trip—trying to be celibate. Those folks in the 'hood didn't get life without sex. I remember their jive talk: 'Can you believe this dude? Can't have no pussy! Hey brudder! We know some stone foxes that'll give you a little leg—no obligation.' Yeah Allan that was hard." I couldn't bring myself to tell Allan about losing my virginity to that beautiful Latina organizer.

I entered the Jesuits in 1963. Ten years later I was finishing my stint as a community organizer on the Near West Side of Chicago's Public Housing Projects. The sounds of "soul music" had replaced Gregorian chant: action overshadowed contemplation; secularity trumped spirituality. My life had moved from the protections and practices of semi-monastic, intellectual institutions to the boiling pot of humanity in the ghetto. I found another photo. I was standing in an abandoned, rubble-filled lot. No clerical garb. Sunglasses. A black jacket, Levi's, hiking boots. Black beard, disheveled, wind-blown hair. I looked like a thug. Those past three years of confrontational organizing had driven me into a hard cynicism. We were spent heroes. A fellow Jesuit from the Dominican Republic, described us as oysters—tough on the outside, soft inside.

There was certainly a heroic quality about being a Jesuit. It got rather confused as that heroism was juxtaposed to the third degree of humility of the crucified Christ figure. I was too young to assimilate the paradox that I am still trying to understand now. I got lost wandering those streets. I thought I could be a messiah on one energetic level, yet on a deeper denied level I had failed. The feeling of calmness in my dissolution and transgression—that peace was a glimpse into what Ignatius called the Contemplation for Obtaining Love.

Now, forty some years later I realize that I was finding a path in that darkness. I thought about all those years of community living at the novitiate in Los Gatos and on the university campuses of Santa Clara, Loyola and Gonzaga. It was a rich life of academics and spiritual practice. I always had insightful, common sense counsel as friends and mentors tried to help me in Ignatius's words: "discern the spirits."

I was attached to the nobler, heroic, messianic idea of the holy man, celibate, above the quagmire, saving everybody: the powerless tenants, the addicts, the young gang members, the prostitutes. It was my attachment, my delusion. St. Ignatius would have counseled me to let go of it; too much dissonance orchestrated by a fearful clinging ego.

I would find my way. The Buddhist mantra came to me—*Om mane padme hum*—the lotus flower emerging out of the mud. I clumsily answered Allan, "Faith is more than faith. I don't know if you can really lose it." Was it Buddha nature or grace that was always there regardless of our delusions? I must have looked befuddled. Allan was like the Zen roshi asking about my koan. In a heartfelt emotion. Allan released me, "Of course, I understand, Mike."

Mike Johnson (California Province 1963–73) with his family—wife, brother and sister-in-law—founded La Chiripada Winery in the Embudo Valley of northern New Mexico near Taos. Last year, 2013, was their thirty-third harvest. He grows grapes, makes wine, and paints. Fifty years ago he picked his first grapes at the vineyards of the Novitiate Winery under the scrutiny of his mentor Father Henri Charvet, SJ.

Falling in Love

Robert Blair Kaiser

When I was a six-year-old in Detroit, I had an unpleasant encounter with a nun with a thick Polish accent. To me, then (I was not yet a Catholic), the Church was a foreign thing. When I landed quite by accident in the eighth grade at St. Francis Xavier in Phoenix, I found the BVM sisters spoke slangy, All-American English, and made me feel I was part of an important family. That that mattered to me then is, in retrospect, a lesson now—that how the faith is presented to us, and by whom, is more important than the "substance" of the faith as summarized in the Creed. If Sister Mary St. Eleanor had told me there were four persons in God, I would have said, "Okay, if you say so."

It wasn't the Creed that got me to the baptismal font that Holy Saturday morning in 1944. It was Sister Mary St. Eleanor's approval and the goodness of my Catholic classmates. My classmates were more "real" to me because they (the boys at least) peppered their speech with "hells" and "damns" whereas the counselors at a Baptist summer camp I attended at the age of twelve wouldn't say "shit" if they had a mouthful. They seemed phony.

The Catholics at St. Francis Xavier (including the Jesuits who ran things there) were real. They helped me grow. Sister Mary St. Eleanor taught me stuff. The young Jesuit priest who coached my (undefeated) eighth grade basketball team, Richard O'Rourke, showed me an effective zone defense.

Later, when I boarded at Loyola High in Los Angeles, the Jesuit priests and the happy scholastics helped me have life and have it more abundantly. I served daily Mass, but I think I was only going through the motions of being a Catholic.

I had to go through the month-long Exercises of St. Ignatius before I began to own my "faith in Jesus," and, even then, that faith was embodied in following daily Common Order: two meditations, two Examens, whips and chains, silence all day, evening litanies, and the Grand Silence at night. My talks with Jesus were one-way conversations. (I had no visions.) But I learned a sense of God's constant presence, helping me Do My Best and understanding me and not being mad at me when I screwed up. Somewhere along the line, I realized it was okay to be human and that I didn't hurt God when I sinned; I hurt myself.

I was never much of a professional at prayer. I liked Ignatius's application of the five senses, taking myself into scenes of Jesus's life, for example, in the cave at Bethlehem, or at Calvary or Emmaus, and I never gave it a thought that the Scriptural accounts might not be "historically true." They worked for me. They helped me be a better Jesuit—that is, more generous in "serving Jesus" by helping others be all they could be.

This was fairly easy when I was a Scholastic at SI, teaching seniors how to write short stories, or coaching JV football. I loved the action, and didn't do a lot of contemplation, but I always felt God's presence (and still do). I liked being a part of a community that celebrated the Christian traditions, feeling grateful in front of the crèche on Christmas Eve, tearing up when I hear Jesus's parable of the Prodigal Son, having my heart burn within me with the disciples at Emmaus.

When I left the Society after Regency, I was still a Jesuit at heart. I tried to see God in all things and appreciate the beauty that surrounded me, including, eventually, the beauty and the love of several good women. This was a pleasant surprise, considering the fear of women programmed into me by my Master of Novices—which stayed with me for too many years. "My transitions?" From brunettes, to blondes, to redheads, to blondes, to brunettes.

Like many men, I guess, I am defined by my loves, but those loves haven't changed that much from my youth to my old age. I love reading good stories and writing good stories and having written good stories. I love trout fishing, I love watching football on TV, I love long lunches with friends, I love cooking and entertaining, I love family dinners, most particularly with my three adult children and my six grandchildren. Through these so-called "created loves," I hope I am getting closer to the Creator of those loves, but I don't think this means I "know God." With Karl Rahner, I believe "God is and always will be incomprehensible mystery, even when we see him face to face."

I like what Father Pedro Arrupe once said about falling in love, and his words ring true to me even when I apply them to my less-than-transcendental life. "What you are in love with, what seizes your imagination, will affect everything. It will decide what will get you out of bed in the morning, what you do with your evenings, how you spend your weekends, what you read, who you know, what breaks your heart, and what amazes you with joy and gratitude. Fall in love, stay in love, and it will decide everything."

After almost ten years in the Jesuits, Robert Blair Kaiser (California Province 1948–57) became a newspaper reporter in Phoenix, then a foreign correspondent in Rome for Time *magazine. He is the author of sixteen published works, five of them on the Church. He has three adult children and six grandchildren. He lives alone in Phoenix, and when he is not writing, he watches football games on TV.*

Gratitude

E. Paul Kelly

The Society of Jesus allowed me to enter and stay for eight years: two as a novice, one as a junior, two in philosophy and the last three in regency. During regency I came to realize I should ask for permission to leave the Society. There were two months of counseling and prayer, ending in a release from vows. The Society stunned me with the gift of a scholarship to law school as I was walking out the door.

Within two weeks of that change in my life, my brother arranged a blind date. Jean and I married each other, two years later. We are blessed with a family of four sons, all of whom are now in their fifties; two of them provided us with grandchildren, two girls, one boy.

In 1960 I began the practice of law in New Hampshire. I joined Jean in being active in our parish church, but the doubts that led to my return to life as a layman had taken deep hold, and little by little I stopped practicing Roman Catholicism, content enough to drop the adjective Roman and pretend, if only to myself, that I was Catholic.

A major turning point came in the 1970s, when I was attracted to Eastern simplicity, particularly in Zen Buddhism, although keenly aware that I could not become a Buddhist simply by wishing it to be so. With the help of Jesuits in Japan, where I spent regency, I learned to practice a Zen-type meditation by sitting and being still, without becoming formally a Buddhist or Taoist or any other Eastern version of what is beyond reason, or rather, the foundation of reason.

A change in my mind-soul came along after many years of this type of meditation: God can do whatever God wants, because God is God. Who am I to judge what others say about God? "Sit and be still and know that I am God."

Retirement from the practice of law came in 2000. I was suddenly lost, without much to do. When the sex abuse of minors broke into the news a couple of years later, my first reaction was that I could now make a formal departure from Catholicism, mostly because I felt a deep insincerity in not being true to myself—or to God.

Astonishingly, I could not do so. So, my desire was to bring the two parts of my life together. I thought that in retirement I could put them together: the Jesuit years and those as a lawyer. I began by writing pieces aimed at renewing the Church, tackling dogmas, decrees and dire pronouncements of hierarchs ending with *"anathema sit."*

After moving from group to group, Compañeros and I found each other. An online community was being offered to me. Tired of struggling alone and lost. I began to share what I thought was going on in my mind-soul, while paying rapt attention to what other members were sharing about themselves. I knew I was home.

While such a community of friends brings with it peace and understanding, it does not necessarily offer a library of learned treatises by spiritual geniuses for me to read and understand and pass along to family and friends. Sitting and being still never attracted me to become a preacher. It was a way of praying quietly, simply, and has been with me for forty years. I wanted to join the two distinct parts of my life to help in renewing the Church, the People of God. The old doubts started to slip away. I stopped arguing with myself and began to share with others.

E. Paul Kelly

Recently, Jean and I were in downtown Portland, Maine. When she went in a large store, I stayed in the car, listening to the radio, which was broadcasting a large choir singing one hymn after the other, even some in Gregorian chant. I was gripped by the music. Every single one of the hymns were what we had sung sixty years before in the choir of our New England Province, and in which I was one of the second tenors for five years.

Sitting alone in the car for over forty-five minutes, humming along, hitting the right notes, but woefully forgetful of the Latin lyrics, I realized I was still Catholic. When Jean returned, I was in tears.

That felt gratitude is with me still: for everything the Jesuits and then my family have given me to be fully human, fully alive.

Paul Kelly (New England Province 1949–57) was born January 16, 1929. He grew up in Dorchester, Massachusetts, attended Boston College, 1949–1960: AB, MA, JD; married Jean Dwyer in 1959. He is a husband, father, grandfather, has four sons, three grandchildren. He was a lawyer in New Hampshire 1960–2000. In retirement, he lived in Colorado and Oregon, discovering the West. Now, he and Jean live in Saco, Maine.

The Link That Binds All Together

Michael E. Kennedy, SJ

One year ago, eleven Jesuit novices and I washed the feet of twelve youth who were incarcerated in Sylmar Juvenile Hall. Almost at the same time Pope Francis was washing the feet of twelve youth locked up in juvenile hall in Rome.

The youth at Sylmar wrote letters to the Pope speaking about the jungle of violence where they live and the constant presence of gangs. This is what he sent back to us after reading the letters to the youth in Rome: "I was very moved to read the letters you sent to me from the young people of Juvenile Hall and to know that we were close to one another in spirit during the washing of feet on Holy Thursday evening. Please tell the young people that I am remembering them in my prayers to our Lord Jesus, who loves each of them with all his heart. I ask them to pray for me and for the needs of all God's people throughout the world. With gratitude and affection I send my blessing. From the Vatican, 12 April 2013, Francis."

Francis's spirit is the spirit of gratitude. Gratitude is what connects all the transitions in my life.

Gratitude is the link between each segment in my faith journey in so many countries, in so many experiences of God working in His people.

The link in the chain that gives birth to gratitude is the word "wisdom."

The Link That Binds All Together

Today in 2014, I am grateful that I am able to give the Spiritual Exercises to those who are locked up in juvenile halls and in state prisons. I am grateful that I can bring the collective wisdom I have gleaned from refugees, immigrants, prisoners, and many other great teachers from the streets. I am grateful in this present transition that I have time to feel this wisdom flow. I am grateful that I am not beginning the journey like the novices I live with, but rather that I can draw from the reservoirs of lived experiences that leave traces of wisdom. This brings consolation to my spirit.

Mike Kennedy, SJ, (California Province 1966)—who goes by Miguel on the streets—lives in Los Angeles and works with the marginalized members of society.

David the "Matchmater"
San Francisco, 1980

John B. Leira

He opened with a large and expansive greeting.

"JOHN! How NICE to see ya! Come INNNN! My, dear, I'd never know you were a priest! You don't look like a priest! You look like a truck driver!"

"Do you lift weights?" he said, scanning me.

David was a five foot nine inch man, stocky, with big-framed black glasses. He had gray hair turning white with a Van Dyke beard. He waddled a bit as he led me down to his office.

The phone rang.

"Excuse me," he said.

"Hello, this is David ," he rattled off.

"Yes . . ."

"Did you like him?"

"Yes . . ."

David then took a card and started writing.

"Listen, dear. I've got to go. I've got someone in my office. Call me when you see Richard. I think you'll really like him. He's an engineer. Very butch. Not too hairy. Just your type," and hung up.

"Now tell me you're not a priest! All of the ones I've met are so nelly! You could put a dress on some of them, and they'd swish."

"Dear, you definitely wouldn't look good in drag."

I laughed, liking this guy.

I liked that he was completely outside of my world.

We spent the next two hours with my answering a series of questions, intimate, but reasonable. His

David the "Matchmater"

focus was on what brought people together. He said that he was old-fashioned and believed in romance.

He explained his former life in Los Angeles as a casting director, matching actors to character roles and as a fashion designer.

"Now I match gay men."

"But dear, I'm the shoeless cobbler. I've still not been able to find the right romantic match for myself." He sighed. "Oh, well, let's get back to you and my service."

He then explained his special procedure, after taking my picture and setting up a file on me.

He explained that I would never see a photograph. He would describe the person and that person's interests.

"People always try to choose from just looks. If I shared pictures, then everyone would pick the good-looking ones."

"I match 'in kind'," he said.

He said that none of his clients were unemployed or retired. "They all want a relationship; not a date like everyone else these days."

He pulled file boxes of 3"x5" cards, marked separately, and then gave me names and descriptions of five people to get me started.

I was to call that person and say, "David gave me your phone number." That was enough.

"You then set up a time to get together and NOT have your first meeting in a bar."

This was about "chemistry."

Later I learned more.

"I file alcoholics and liars in my "hell" file, and then they all meet each other."

He snickered, and I laughed.

"I'm a dictator," he continued. "I put people where they belong."

"Everybody wants the cutest man in town, but I always say, 'You can always get a piece of ass but not necessarily peace of mind.'"

"Always be selective with whom you're erective!" and "You don't match two exclusive anal passives."

He was irreverent and said things that were direct and hostile toward religion, like, describing an agnostic as opposed to atheists.

"If you sit on the fence, you get a picket up your ass."

"It's all superstition. I don't believe in a deity."

"I'm Jewish. Was even raised Orthodox."

We then took care of finances.

"Well, then, John, you're set."

"No hurt feelings here. It's all compatibility. There are many fish in the sea, John. I've been around a long time."

We concluded and he showed me back to the door.

"We're going to be just fine, dear."

"They'd never believe you were a priest. But it could be a turn on! 'Forbidden fruit!' Ha!"

"Lot's of fish, dear. Lots of fish."

I returned to my car as the late afternoon fog rolled around me, cooling me.

For the first time in years I finally no longer felt alone.

Eventually I found my match, and we're in our thirtieth year together.

John Leira (California Province 1965–87) has taught high school classes, given retreats, and worked with a wide range of people who always remain interesting to him. He lives and writes with verve and humor. He currently is studying Literature at the University of San Francisco, a city John and his partner Jerry know well and love deeply. John is an accomplished chef and a supporter of the Arts in the Bay Area.

The Look of Mary Robillard

Raymond J. Leonardini

In the spring of 1961, I was a senior at St. Ignatius High School in San Francisco. At that time a notorious killer was awaiting execution in San Quentin's gas chamber. Two years previously, Alex Robillard was stopped in a stolen car by Hillsborough police officer Eugene Doran. Alex was nineteen at the time and a professional criminal. He shot Doran six times, the last bullet fired in the neck to ensure death.

I knew of the pending execution. Everybody did. In those days I had no opinion about the death penalty. I never gave it much thought. It didn't impact me at all until Fr. John Enright, SJ, called me out of English class on April 25, 1961.

John Enright was a sophomore Religion teacher and spiritual counselor at St. Ignatius. He asked me to be a pall-bearer for the funeral of Alex Robillard, who was to be executed the next day. It seems Fr. Enright had written to Robillard while he was awaiting execution, asked him if he wanted to talk to him. He did, and there started an intense relationship ending with Fr. Enright hearing his confession and witnessing his execution.

I was nervous and intimidated on the day of the funeral. The five other pall-bearers were classmates and we had a sinking feeling in our stomachs as we rode in the limo behind the hearse. We did not know what to expect.

Because of Fr. Enright's involvement, the funeral was held at the old Oakland Cathedral. I had never seen it. The outline of its Gothic architecture was barely visible because all the lights in the cavernous church were turned off. It was ominous. Way off in the distance we could make out the altar with the

The Look of Mary Robillard

family standing to one side. We slowly processed up toward the altar. No music, the cathedral totally empty except for the family, John Enright, and we six pall-bearers.

Robillard's mother seemed to be tending to her husband, two sons, and daughter, shielding them in some fashion, perhaps trying to protect them from the coming rituals. As we stopped at the altar rail, she looked directly at me.

She had a fractured look of inconsolable sadness and heartache. Yet, as she looked at me, I could also see her offering me an unmistakable gratefulness. I was stunned. The combination of grief and gratefulness confused me. I felt embarrassed that until that moment I had not made the connection that Alex Robillard had a mother.

Over the years I have thought about Mary Robillard many times, with increasing gratitude for her special gift to me. She has become an inspiration. By holding her pain in the unique fashion that she did, she wordlessly brought me to a deeper consciousness of the transformative power of her suffering.

Ray Leonardini (California Province 1961–70) is a former lawyer who practiced government and nonprofit law for nearly thirty years. After his retirement he turned toward his foremost area of interest: the Christian spiritual journey. For the last five years, as a Volunteer Chaplain, he has led prayer groups and taught Contemplative Meditation and the Spiritual Journey at Folsom State Prison in California. He is also the Director of the Prison Contemplative Fellowship, an association of current and former prison inmates committed to reaching out to prisoners and their families on their travels along the spiritual path.

The Primacy of Intuition

John LeSarge

I left the Canadian Province of the Society of Jesus in the spring of 1981. After years of passionate service in the ministry of the *Spiritual Exercises* of St. Ignatius, I found myself drained of all desire to continue my work. I began to search for reasons why. I never lost the presence of God but he was so distant. I continually asked him what he was saying that I was not hearing? But seemingly I received no answer. This went on for two years until I finally in anger told God that I felt like a puppet on the end of a string. I told him that I have only two absolutes in my life: God himself and my Jesuit vocation. At that moment I was struck with such a powerful grace that I was knocked from my chair to my prie-dieu. I asked: "Are you asking me to leave the Society?" At that moment I was filled with unspeakable peace and joy. I knew that I would leave the Society. However, I soon came down from this peak experience and glimpsed the challenge that lay ahead. I then said: "Lord, I am frightened at what lies ahead. The Lord responded: 'trust me'!".

After my encounter with Our Lord, I left the domestic chapel and headed for the University Chapel. On my way I met the woman who eventually became my wife. I invited her to join me in a celebration of the Holy Eucharist. There was no romantic involvement between us at this time. When I read the gospel for that day, the following words took hold of her and me: "An angel of the Lord appeared to him (Joseph) in a dream and said, 'Joseph, son of David, do not be afraid to take Mary as your wife'" (Matt. 1:20).

Eileen and I were most embarrassed because we both acknowledged that we had heard the same message: "John, take Eileen as your wife." I immediately suggested that we test the spirit of this suggestion, or was it a command? We separated for six months. I left for Toronto while Eileen remained in Winnipeg. Eileen left her religious congregation three months later. I returned to Toronto, and in six months I returned to Winnipeg. We were married and through the years that followed our love for each other deepened, as did our trust in our heavenly Father. We began to understand what the Lord meant when he said 'Trust Me."

I had no desire to continue in the Roman Catholic Church. As Rodriguez would say, there were "various and sundry reasons" why. However, there was one reason that stood out: Pope John Paul II said any ex-priest must wait five years before he can apply for a dispensation to re-enter. Eileen and I had to get on with our lives and we needed a faith community.

When Eileen and I were admitted into the Anglican Communion, Archbishop Walter Jones greeted us with kindness and said: "I hope that you continue from where you are." In the years to follow Walter treated us as he greeted us. I don't think that he was aware of how much his acceptance meant to Eileen and me.

The Anglican community builds its spirituality around three pillars: Scripture, Tradition, and Reason. There is no mention of Religious Experience. This puzzled me until I found an article that recorded a controversy between William James and John Henry Newman. It was a controversy that pitted reason against feelings. James wrote:

"(That part of man's life) of which rationalism can give an account is relatively superficial. It is the part that has the prestige undoubtedly, for it has the loquacity, it can challenge you for proofs, and chop logic, and put you down with words.

But it will fail to convince or convert you all the same, if your dumb intuitions are opposed to its conclusions. If you have intuitions at all, they come from a deeper level of your nature than the loquacious level which rationalism inhabits."

For the most part Newman agreed with James; however, he took issue over the statement that his notional and real assent gives primacy to reason over feelings. James contends that intellectual operations only interpret the feelings. First there are feelings, then an intellectual interpretation that is independent or comes after the feelings.

Newman, however, was saying that there is no such thing as an experience composed merely of feelings; there is always an intelligible content. Secondly, an intellectual interpretation is not an intrusion into experience but is simply bringing to understanding the meaning implicit in the experience itself.

I like to put this in Lonerganian terms that make a distinction between knowledge and meaning. Meaning is a much broader term than knowledge and includes knowledge. As T. S. Eliot said: "We had the experience but missed the meaning." To grasp the meaning in the experience is what spiritual direction is all about.

Eileen and I gave ourselves to the ministry of word and sacrament within our parish community. This brought us many blessings. We also grew in appreciation of Christian tradition through study and contemplation of Christian art and architecture. Eileen passed away in 2009, but her loving spirit, of course, lingers in my continuing life.

John LeSarge (English Canada Province 1953–81) is a retired Anglican priest living in Canada.

Roads Taken

John B. Lounibos

My first spiritual transition came at age twenty when I left a lifetime spent living and working on twenty-five acres of poultry ranch, west of Petaluma, Sonoma County, California, working for six years harvesting hay on two dairy ranches, to join the Jesuits at Los Gatos, California. Fortunately I remained engaged in products of nature as we harvested grapes for the Novitiate Winery for four years. Leaving home and our family of nine to follow Christ more closely with the three vows of religion, motivated by the *Spiritual Exercises* of St. Ignatius Loyola, maintained two other continuities: sacramental-liturgical life, and academic studies. Many other things changed, especially a prayer life.

My second spiritual transition consisted of achieving a strong sense of responsibility teaching Latin and English, coaching two sports, prefecting fifty senior boarders, maintaining and driving buses for three years for the students at Bellarmine College Preparatory in San Jose, California. On Sundays I took Sodality members to entertain patients at the nearby Agnews State Mental Hospital. Character building accompanied spiritual development.

A third spiritual transition took place in the early 1960s. Continual reports from the Second Vatican Council (1962–65) motivated me to change my major academic interest from philosophy (BA, MA), begun at USF (1952–54), to theology. Maybe the plan to begin four years of theological studies after teaching helped inspire this change.

A fourth spiritual transition took place in the late '60s when Alma College invited Carl Rogers and colleagues to conduct a weekend workshop for theologians. Many of us consciously profited from emotional awakenings. My book, which was inspired by that experience, *Changes in the Church*, completed in 1968, lies fallow—unpublished.

A fifth spiritual transition came with my pilgrimage to Europe to study German with three other Jesuits, and complete the required third year of religious study—tertianship—in Italy. Now I could read and understand some French, German, and Italian. It has helped me read *Catholic New York's* Spanish sections. Roles as civilian Chaplain for the US Army at Leighton Barracks, Würzburg, Germany, and Camp Darby, Livorno, Italy, were life-expanding.

A sixth transition came as I exited the Society of Jesus after seventeen years, to begin raising a family and teach Religious Studies at Dominican College of Blauvelt, New York (1971–2007). The Christ gestalt of a community shifted to the Christ gestalt of a soul-mate. Anne Marie and I are proud parents of Mark Daniel and Kristin Anne, with their spouses and five grandchildren, Sophia, Elena, Lucy, Henry, and Daniel. These changes impact not just my spirit, but also our local, national, and world cultures in ways we can scarcely fathom.

John Lounibos (California Province 1954–71) and his wife Anne Marie live in Blauvelt, New York. He continues to research and comment on subjects popular and arcane to the delight of many who await his explanations on the Compañeros listserv.

A.M.D.G.

Kathleen M. MacPherson

My family is half-Irish, half-Italian/Mexican, and almost all nominal Catholic. A formidable Jesuit educational background helped me to come to grips with a chromosomal birth defect. Therapy and counseling brought me to a point in my early life when I was able to accept myself as the Creator had composed me from all eternity.

Jesuit education helped me to overcome diversity and perceived handicaps, and focus on a life filled with service with and through the Church. These confusing early years created in me a tremendous empathy for the less fortunate and marginalized members of society.

I left Spokane in 1968 to teach Spanish at Loyola High School in Los Angeles. It was similar to going to high school all over again. The only difference, this time, was that I had the grade book in my hand.

In the summer of 1969, I went to Mexico City to study at the University of the Americas for an intensive summer of Spanish language, culture, and history. I associated with a group of Jesuits in Mexico who were deeply concerned with the plight of the marginalized in society, and to prove their point, they closed the most affluent and prestigious college preparatory school in all of Mexico and probably in all of Latin America, Instituto Patria.

In 1971, I transferred to the Jesuit Instituto Carlos Pereyra in Torreon, Coahuila, to teach ESL (English as a Second Language). I learned far more than what I taught. The people, parents, and students showed me a different reflection of myself. To the present day, I have never enjoyed anything as much as teaching there, although there were some missteps.

A.M.D.G.

The following year, I went to Mexico City to study theology at the Instituto Libre de Filosofia, the Jesuit theologate in Mexico City. I studied at the Jesuit School of Theology in Mexico City from 1971 to 1973 with an excellent faculty.

I met my future spouse in México, and life became focused: teaching, family, and two pregnancies. We stayed in Mexico until 1978 when the Golden Gate lured us back to the United States. Work with the San Francisco Police Department led me to pursue a Doctor of Jurisprudence degree with a Master's in Public Administration, specializing in the Administration of Justice.

Life on the streets of San Francisco brought me cheek to cheek with the harsh reality of excruciating pain and suffering in the everyday life of human beings brought on by sin and hatred and loss of true volition due to drug and alcohol addiction.

During many a midnight session in smelly alleyways and overcrowded emergency rooms, I never realized that I would become a priest-chaplain in a county hospital, in Texas working almost daily in Intensive Care into the twenty-first century.

In law school, I studied under Bernard Segal, Robert Calhoun, and a host of other legal scholars who were both legal academicians and everyday practitioners. I discovered that the everyday living out of the gospels and theology had to reach the most despised and forgotten of society, those accused of crimes punishable by imprisonment.

I left Texas in 2002 for Virginia because the Lone Star state had become claustrophobic. It turned out that I wanted to leave more than just San Antonio. My spouse died after a twenty-year bout with manic depression that devastated mind and body. I then discovered another spiritual practice, which does a whole lot to shape perception, emotions, and identity: the practice of total service to the community.

In Virginia Beach, Virginia, I had some lengthy conversations with two priests who came down from Richmond in 2005. Both were civil lawyers and canon lawyers of the Church. After some very engaging discussions with them, I felt a tremendous calling and took all my theology, Spanish, and lawyering to Washington, DC, to become a canon lawyer at the faculty of the Catholic University of America, the only canon law faculty in the United States. In Washington, DC, I found myself counseling drug addicts and alcoholics at DuPont Circle in downtown Washington, preparing witnesses in the witness protection program for in-court testimony through the Department of Justice, and authoring the best half of my life story.

After ordination to the priesthood in the Independent Catholic tradition, I now work with so many immigrants, convicts, drug addicts, politicians, and people whom I have counseled as a teacher and a lawyer who are waiting for me not just to speak to them about theology and law, but are looking at me to find the sacramental Jesus Christ and the triune God in the Eucharist and the sacraments. Being a priest to me means bringing the incarnate and sacramental Christ into the lives of those who do not even realize that God is speaking to them through me.

Rev. Kathleen M. MacPherson, MDiv, JD, Pastor and Director, St. Oscar Romero Pastoral and Outreach Center, El Paso, Texas, USA & Ciudad Juarez, Chihuahua, Mexico

A Grief Delayed

G. Donald Maloney

My journey to, in, and out of the Jesuit order would take many words. The oldest of four children born to an Irish-American Catholic family in San Francisco, I was very religious as a youngster, praying constantly, serving at early morning Masses, etc. I visited St. Joseph's Minor Seminary in Mountain View during the eighth grade and talked to my parents about attending. My mother felt (rightly) that I was not mature enough for such a decision and asked that I attend high school for a couple of years and then consider the seminary. At this time, I idolized my father, a successful attorney, but was emotionally closer to my mother.

From this point on I would divide my life into two tracks, the emotional and the theological. Both are inevitably intertwined but the distinction makes sense to me. In my first year at St. Ignatius, my mother was diagnosed with a mysterious illness—she had surgery, and recuperated in the French Hospital on Geary Blvd. I remember taking the streetcar to visit her after my school day at SI. After a sudden coma, she awoke feeling better and came home for Thanksgiving, Christmas, and a New Year's week-end at our place on the Russian River. On January 2nd I returned to school only to have my father come to tell me that my mother was in a coma again. I visited her once when she was in the coma and felt helpless and lost. I prayed desperately that she would live. She died on January 13, 1949. I was unprepared for her loss. I did not cry at the funeral or burial, and kept repeating to myself and to others the mantra "It is God's will and therefore for the best." I did not know how to grieve and got no help from those dealing with their own loss. Only in retrospect have I come to understand what was going on in me. I was, I now know, afraid that my feelings of irreversible loss would overwhelm my fragile self. And so I steeled myself, trying to act like "a man." The result was a deadening of feeling and a strange detachment from my family and life in general. I also felt guilt and a lack of joy about life.

During the ensuing high-school years I was successful in studies and sports and had two or three loyal girlfriends. On the surface I seemed quite normal, but inside I felt emotionally detached from everyone, had strong guilt feelings and anxiety. My father married again a year and a half after my mother's death and I began an uncomfortable and complicated relationship with my stepmother, resisting with passive aggression. I found it disturbingly easy to leave my father, brother, and sisters to enter Los Gatos after my senior year.

It was at Los Gatos that I experienced the "bait and switch" tactic of Fr. Master Healy, which only fed into my guilt and anxiety. What was this tactic? Well, most of us were thinking that by entering the novitiate we were "exploring" a vocation. Fr. Healy, however, told us that our acceptance as novices was proof that we definitely had a vocation and our only option was to accept God's call, or turn our backs on it—hardly a welcome dilemma for guilt-laden and insecure adolescents. Of course, the Society could end my "vocation" by dismissing me. The freedom was all on their side. At this point I decided (not exactly happily) that I could never leave the Society without rejecting God in some way. I also experienced a devaluing of any prior spiritual life I had as a child and young man. Such spirituality was immature, I intuited, and now I would start afresh with real spiritual development.

However, I have no regret whatsoever for my life as a Jesuit—twenty-eight years. And I don't mean to be hard on Jim Healy. I lived with him at Bellarmine during his days as a hypnotist, and made a retreat with him when I was thinking of taking a leave of absence. Both he and I were victims of a faulty spiritual theology during the early 1950s.

After juniorate at Los Gatos I went to the Mount. Taking private psychology courses from Jack Evoy, SJ, helped me to understand my life to some extent, and I was impressed by how normal and down-to-earth Jack was as a person. Fr. Frank Marien was both my teacher and occasional spiritual director and was the first to notice that I had intellectualized the loss of my mother, blocking the emotional impact. But he didn't get through to me.

My regency at Bellarmine was busy and challenging. The photos of me in the student catalogues tell the story—unsmiling, cold, aloof. That's how I felt inside. I had little positive feeling about myself and was mildly depressed. But at least I could look forward to the next step, which would get me away from California. Although I got along with all my fellow Jesuits, I had no special attachment to them or to the area, and was pleased to be assigned to Weston for theology.

Something had to give, and it did. During my third year of theology, I was lying on my bed one day reviewing my life to get some insight into why and how I started feeling so negatively about myself and life. Early memories surfaced from my childhood, and in all of them was the feeling of my mother's presence—steady and loving. I saw her humor and vibrant personality. Suddenly my inner defenses crumbled and the tears came pouring out. I was deeply sorrowful for what I had lost. I cried for three days, interrupted only by meals. When I finally was composed, I sensed that something very significant was happening within me, and I felt at peace.

I also experienced a closeness to God that I had had as a child and adolescent, and felt free in a way I had not felt before. I was flawed and weak in many ways, but God loved me. This was a turning point in my life. I was fortunate to have as spiritual director Fr. Dan Shine, who recognized that I had had an important breakthrough, and who was wise enough to avoid interpreting the experience with some pious platitude. Something in me had changed radically but what emerged did not seem new but familiar, and from an earlier time in my life.

I was ordained, a step I have never regretted. and felt genuine as a priest, although I was seriously put off by the pomp of my first Solemn Mass.

During theology I had discovered Karl Rahner, reading everything of his I could get. His theological reflections seemed to mesh well with my new freedom to think in new ways about what was being taught, and I began being my own theologian. I was assistant Newman Club chaplain at Brandeis in Waltham in my fourth year of theology, and taught a New Testament course at Holy Cross. At Weston I had an opening of mind and heart.

In 1966 I headed to Europe for tertianship at Wepion, Belgium, and for four months was the Catholic chaplain at a US Army base in Germany. One of the side-effects of my new freedom was that I now felt no guilt in following my natural attraction to women.

At the base I had a minor romantic relationship with one of the American teachers (with whom I am still in occasional contact). After tertianship I enrolled in the doctoral program at Strasbourg but immediately went to Muenster, Germany, to take Rahner's courses and to prepare my thesis. I returned to Strasbourg after a year to write my doctoral thesis, which I defended on November 29th, 1969. During these years I had a few relationships with women and a serious one with a German student whom I met in Strasbourg. She is still a friend.

G. Donald Maloney

I was assigned to LMU (then Loyola U.) and in 1970 became chair of the theology department. Tom Higgins was my best friend at LMU and we supported each other during many difficult times. I was a good and caring priest but my behavior with women was certainly questionable. I had relationships with some female students, a few of them intimate, and realized that I had to make a decision about my life. Strangely I had no guilt about the relationships but recognized that there was an obvious contradiction in how I was living. I was quite open in my behavior and almost wanted to be caught.

In 1976 I was offered final vows, and decided to take a leave of absence. I joined a diocesan volunteer group in Colorado and was a teacher and Newman Club Chaplain at Mesa College in Grand Junction. After that, I joined VISTA and worked for two years in Ely, Nevada. I then returned to teaching in San Diego before joining the University of Maryland in Europe. I went to Europe with a woman I had met in San Diego but the relationship did not work out. In 1982 I met my wife, Paula, in Spain where I was teaching at the time. She had two young children, five and two, and was in the process of separating from her husband. She and I have been married now going on twenty-six years. I am still praying, believing, and hoping. I have never been laicized (don't believe in it) and am conscious of being a priest. I am deeply grateful for my life as it has been, and is. I pray daily that I might be a channel of grace to those I come in contact with, and not an obstacle.

Don Maloney (California Province 1952–82) and his wife Paula live in Golden, Colorado, though they have taught and worked in medical venues in Okinawa, Japan, and elsewhere. The last five sentences in Don's contribution are an informal biography. He is who he is.

Bus 68

John McConville

I was on a bus in Bangkok. I was twenty-six years old. I was on my way to language school traveling there from Victory Monument where the Jesuit Residence, Xavier Hall, was established. Union Language School was on the eighth floor of the now defunct Silom Building. I had been in language school for six months, and I took Bus 68 every morning for a thirty-minute ride to the busy financial district on Silom Road.

It was early November 1974, and the monsoon rains had suddenly stopped. The weather was now in the low 80s, and the breeze was cooler than usual—a relief from the high 90s and the oppressive humidity.

The bus was packed as usual, and I was hanging onto a bar attached to the ceiling at the back of the bus. The ride was bumpy, and I was being thrown back and forth by the quick stops and starts as were all the other passengers on their way to work this Monday morning.

I enjoyed these early morning rides. Thai people, I discovered, were very comfortable standing close to each other and were quite free in touching each other (men with men, women with women), holding hands, sitting on one another's laps, walking arm in arm. It was on these early morning bus rides that I had the pleasure of people pressed against me and felt perhaps for the first time how nice it was to be touched even if it was unintentional and fleeting; even if it was an accidental brush up against my chest or a squeeze of my rear end as someone was pushing to make room.

I had just come through a very dark six months of being the only Jesuit Scholastic in a residence of very independent Jesuit priests, four from Spain, two from Italy, one from the USA, one from Canada, and one saintly old man from France who made his home in Klong Toery, the slums of Bangkok. Living with these Jesuits, I was truly cut off from the world in a way I had never been before. My lifeline to people, language, the familiarity of food, sounds, smells and gestures had vanished, and I felt deeply alone. Shortly after my arrival in Thailand I fell into a terrible depression, something my ritual of prayer and daily Mass did not seem to address. I was unable to share my experience of loneliness and depression with my spiritual father for fear I would sound lost and (God forbid) unholy. I was afraid of failure. I was afraid I did not have the spiritual strength to be a Jesuit missionary, and I would be sent home disgraced. I was mostly afraid of something I had been afraid of all my life, my gnawing, relentless ever-present and persistent sexual desires. I was attracted to men. I was gay. I kept this a secret, even from myself.

And so, this Monday morning on Bus 68, with the "relatively cool" pleasant weather and the gentle and not-so-gentle pushing and shoving, something happened that I cannot explain. I felt touched in a new and different way, which I have often defined in retrospect as a divine intervention.

Exactly what was different, I do not know, but my mood began to change and the heavy depression seemed to lift, and as I stepped off the bus at the corner of Silom and Saladaeng I felt happy to be alive. My shirt had been unbuttoned and my belt had been undone. Was it just from the jostling of the passengers? I don't remember, but as I put myself together on that street corner, buttoning up my shirt and fixing my belt, I found myself laughing. The sun beamed down on me, and I looked up into the heavens and I screamed, "I am alive!!! I am gay! It's OK!"

What a day of joy that was and one that has influenced me deeply. A sweet and powerful turn into my heart and soul and a profound gratitude for my body given to me out of nothing to live in each and every day. I was assured; the whole of me was HOLY.

John McConville (California Province 1966–80) now resides in Oakland, California and is a spiritual care counselor for hospice as well as a psychotherapist in private practice.

Much More the Jesuit

Douglass D. McFerran

I still have a journal for my final year and a half as a Jesuit. It's a composition book from St. Ignatius High, where I taught algebra to freshmen and Spanish to sophomores and juniors. I still look at it occasionally to remind myself of what I had been going through before and after the fateful visit with the provincial that resulted in my requesting a release from my vows.

I really do not much like the person I find expressing himself. If I could do the time-traveler thing and drop in to chat with that severely introverted scholastic, I would tell him to stop feeling sorry for himself and make the effort to genuinely care about the people around him. No wonder the idea of being a priest was so daunting. He had really missed the point.

What I said to the provincial was really not that different from what I had said to James Healy, my novice master. I did not feel the emotional attachment to the priesthood. I was there because I had completely bought into the concept that it was better to be a priest than a layman, a religious rather than a diocesan priest, and a Jesuit because its training was the longest and arguably the best. For Father Healy this was just a temptation against my vocation. For Carroll O'Sullivan that was definitely not enough. I was not really called to the priesthood if I did not feel it. I should pray about this, maybe even take another year of regency to work things through. A relatively short time later I had made my decision, although even when the papers had come back from Rome, I was asked to stay for the final semester.

It is only recently that I have begun to realize what I may have missed by not going on. When I left the Jesuits I still was the committed believer. I was also, I appreciate, still a mess as far as my head and heart were concerned. It would be years before I managed to come to grips with what had been driving me into a world where, as I find I kept noting in my journal, I never had the feeling that I belonged. What I have learned from years of conversation with those who did go on to theology at Alma is that there at least an effort was being made to enable both psychological and spiritual growth. Maybe I could have been a good and caring priest, after all.

However, I also have to acknowledge that the individual who wrote that journal might have had too hard a time letting go. Much more had to happen before he would be ready to do so. Ironically, it is largely through association with the Companions (reunions and listserv) that much of this would take place a long time after. Where I am today: much less the Catholic but much more the Jesuit, grateful for what I was offered but sorry that I was so unprepared to appreciate it at the time.

Doug McFerran entered the novitiate at Los Gatos in 1952 and left the Jesuits after completing regency at St. Ignatius High in San Francisco ten years later. He went on to private-school and then community-college teaching in Los Angeles, but It would take ten years more before he was willing to talk about his Jesuit past at the time his first book was published. He is now retired from teaching but continues his work as a writer.

A Mudala in Zambia

James P. McGloin, SJ

I was raised in Butte, Montana; Zambia, a country in Southern Africa, has been my home for the past forty years. How did a boy from the copper-mining city of Butte end up in Zambia, one of the largest copper producers in the world? Copper has no magnetic properties so my native copper did not draw me to Zambian copper. Rather it was a more complex transition, the outward circumstances of which are easy to narrate, but what went on inside me is much more difficult to explain.

The journey had a number of steps. The first step was from Butte to the Jesuits. After finishing high school at Butte Central in 1962, ten of us (five young men and five young women) from Central went to Gonzaga University in Spokane, Washington. This was long before the University became known as a basketball powerhouse; at the time, it was a small Catholic liberal arts college. I enjoyed the studies at the University, being away from home, meeting new friends, but especially having the support of good friends from Butte. However, I was uncertain what I wanted to do in the future so I took courses that would fulfill the general requirements for a BA degree. One of the courses I took was a scripture course, an introductory course on St. John's Gospel, from Fr. Joseph Conwell, SJ; the course opened a door to scripture that whetted my appetite for the subject. Although he never taught me, Fr. Jerome ("Judd") Murray from Butte, was always available to help us struggling calculus students from Butte. And Fr. Tim O'Leary, another Butte man, was a larger than life, but caring, figure in DeSmet Hall, the main dormitory for men at the time. (Butte people watch out for each other if you are not aware!) I began to admire the Jesuits on the campus.

Every student had to make a weekend retreat during the academic year. The retreat I attended was at Priest Lake in Northern Idaho; it was winter and the whole area was covered with snow. I enjoyed the whiteness and the silence of the place. During the retreat, I went to confession to the priest (not a Jesuit) who was giving the retreat. Out of the blue he asked me if I had ever thought of a vocation. I told him that in high school I had considered it as a possibility, but that I did not feel called to either the Christian Brothers or the diocesan priesthood, the two groups I had known in Butte, and so I dismissed it. He said I should reconsider the possibility.

And I did reconsider it. I spoke to the chaplain at the University who encouraged me to speak to a few other Jesuits on campus, and he made arrangements for me and other students, also considering the Jesuits, to meet scholastics who were doing their philosophy studies at nearby Mount St. Michael's. I became more impressed. However, indecision remained very much part of my day-to-day life. Finally, just before spring break, I decided I should at least give the Jesuits a try. If it wasn't for me I could leave. But if I didn't at least try, the notion of a "vocation" might continue to haunt me.

In September 1963 I entered the Jesuit novitiate in Sheridan, Oregon, to "try it out." Last year I celebrated fifty years as a Jesuit. Although there have been ups and downs, as in any human life, I'm glad I tried it out. The Jesuit life has been a good "fit" for me, and has given me a spiritual, educational, and apostolic direction to my life.

The next big step was from the USA to Zambia. When I joined the Jesuits, the Oregon Province had been one of the provinces asked by the Superior

James P. McGloin, SJ

General of the Jesuits to help supply men and finances to the Polish mission that had existed in Zambia (previously Northern Rhodesia) since the early 1900s. Because of the Communist takeover of Poland after the war, the Polish Jesuits were no longer able to maintain the mission. Some Oregon Province Jesuits were sent to help, and, in my novitiate fervor, I inquired about the possibility.

I never thought much further about the request. In December 1968, I finished my degree at St. Louis University. Then a topsy-turvy interlude with much uncertainty became part of my life again. At first I was assigned to Jesuit High School in Portland to teach for the next two years. Then, after I had already sent my books and belongings to Portland, the assignment was changed and I was asked to go to Spokane to teach at Gonzaga Prep School. However, shortly before I was due to travel to Spokane, I received a phone call from the Provincial's office in Portland asking me to get a health check-up, because there might be a possibility of being sent to Zambia.

In the late 1960s through much of the 1970s, there was great social upheaval in the United States. This also affected the Catholic Church and, in particular, religious life and priesthood. Many left the priesthood or religious life to get married and pursue other ways of living. We Jesuits were not immune to the disturbance. First a Jesuit companion, who was teaching at Gonzaga Prep, left the Jesuits; for me that meant I'd teach in Spokane. Then the one scheduled to go to Zambia, who had a degree in agricultural science and had shown a real interest in Zambia, asked to leave; for me that meant not Spokane, but Zambia. So I ended up teaching a semester at Gonzaga Prep, but in August, with some fear, but also a sense of adventure, I was on my way to Zambia.

A Mudala in Zambia

In Zambia I was posted to a diocesan secondary school outside of Kabwe, a small mining town (lead and zinc, this time). I liked the supportive community, appreciated the Zambian students and their families, and I was taken by the vibrancy of a young country that had recently become independent.

After two years of teaching, I returned to the States to begin my theology studies in preparation for the priesthood. On my return, I found it much more difficult adjusting to life in the States than I had in adjusting to Zambia. The wealth and waste of the American lifestyle contrasted so much to the simpler life style that I had gotten used to. Eventually I did settle into the life of studies, but I was also certain that I would like to return to Zambia after my ordination. And I did in 1975. Although my original coming to Zambia might have seemed like a fluke, my return was my own deep desire.

I have been here almost continually since then. I have lived and worked in different parts of the country: Kitwe, a copper mining city, Kabwe, Chikuni Mission in rural southern Zambia and in the capital, Lusaka. I have taught in a government high school and in a Jesuit College of Education; I've worked in parishes, been involved in chaplaincy work, given retreats and the complete Spiritual Exercises, and in recent years done administrative work for the Jesuit Province. I've lived in communities with Irish, Polish, Slovenian, Zambian, Malawian, and other African Jesuits. It has been an enlarging experience for me.

In recent years the Society in Zambia has been blessed with solid Jesuit vocations. Now the Zambians and Malawians are the majority of the membership of the Province and are taking over more and more leadership roles. For us expatriates, us "missionaries," this development is a blessing and also a challenge: a blessing knowing that Jesuit life and work will continue; a challenge letting go and letting others take charge.

What about the future? About the past I can look back and remember; about the future, I have no idea. I will leave that in the hands of God. For the moment, however, as long as my health is good and as long as I can make some contribution to the mission here, I'm happy to stay put. I still enjoy what I do; I still appreciate the Zambians I deal with, many of whom are good friends, and, as a senior citizen, a "mudala," I am respected and made to feel at home. As Cardinal Newman once said: "[God] leads us by a strange way, a *mirabilis via*. . . . [God] will bring us to that which is, not indeed what we think best, nor what is best for another, but what is best for us."

Jim McGloin, SJ, (Oregon Province 1963 and Zambia-Malawi Province 1981) is almost 70. He lives in Lusaka and is as busy as ever in the country he loves.

Mystery Ends

Michael G. Merriman

Twenty-five years ago I left the Society of Jesus after thirty-five years. Reflecting on those years gives me the opportunity to thank God and the Society for that time, from the years of formation, ordination, and ministry that has nourished me all the rest of my life.

In looking at my life since I left the Society, I realize that my Jesuit years were the foundation of all that I have done, since the order of these events flow into one another, but can be put into four periods.

First, my fifteen years of marriage to my wife Margaret showed me what it meant to be loved unconditionally and in turn to try and give to her my unconditional love. Margaret died very suddenly eleven years ago. We had just finished saying a rosary because she did not feel well enough to attend Mass that morning. I had poured each of us a drink and she collapsed and died. It was shortly after the words we had just recited, "Now and at the hour of our death."

Second, after I left the Society I went to work for my brother Nick's company in Seattle. However, I needed something more in my life, and took training to be a hospice volunteer at Northwest Hospital in Seattle. After this training, and my background check, I was offered the position as a non-denominational pastoral counselor/chaplain. I served in this position for several years until Margaret burned out as a fund-raiser for non-profits in the Seattle area. We sold our home and—to fulfill a dream—moved to the Oregon coast, building a home in Lincoln City. I became a member of the board of my brother's company in Portland.

I also took the position as chaplain for the North Lincoln Hospital Hospice. Many of the residents moved to the coast to retire. Tragedy strikes (mainly cancer) and they are reluctant to call their former church, or they have no church affiliation and desire spiritual help. I was privileged to do this ministry and found it fulfilling. I became a member of the Oregon State Hospice Association and was part of the opposition to the "right to die movement" which failed to pass on the first round. The ministry was very consoling and Margaret was able to assist me.

Third, after eleven years on the Oregon coast, we moved to Portland. Margaret was in poor health and needed to be closer to more doctors, though they were never able to diagnose her condition. She also had three grown children and grandchildren in Portland. After Margaret died, I became a member of St. Ignatius parish and helped Peter Byrne, SJ, with retreats, days of recollection, etc., etc. After discussion with Peter, I became a staff member as a volunteer for the next ten years. The highlights of these years are difficult to express because they were so many. But the retreat in Spokane at Regis Community with Chuck Peterson, SJ, was special. I was warmly welcomed and received. John Schwarz SJ, made the retreat and died shortly afterwards. I gave his eulogy and recalled our days at Gonzaga, where I was his godfather at his Baptism. We entered the novitiate together in 1951.

Fourth, I was diagnosed with Parkinson's disease six years ago. Shortly before going to Missoula, Montana, to give the Novena of Grace with my close friend, Tom Healy, SJ, I noticed tremors in my hands. I went to the doctor and it was Parkinson's disease. For me, it is progressive and makes me extremely tired. I am doing as well as can be expected, and my doctor told me recently, "You have had a heart attack, four bypasses, Parkinson's disease, and are 84 years old. You are living on borrowed time."

Thus, mystery ends. But it has been a wonderful life. God has been very good to me. All that I am, intellectually, spiritually, materially, and socially is due to my Jesuit years. God has taken good care of me. Now I ask that I can make some return for all that has been given me.

Mike Merriman (Oregon Province 1951–86) resides at Mary's Woods near Marylhurst University in Lake Oswego, Oregon. He stays in touch with Peter Byrne, SJ, and other Jesuit friends.

The Primacy of Desire

Joseph J. Mitchell

Now, as I am beginning this sharing, I am questioning myself: why do I want to share this transition in my life with you? (And, as I reflect, I want to be aware that my ego could get involved here, and I don't want that to be the reason that I am sharing.) My ego probably will get involved. Nonetheless, I want to say clearly, I value sharing this experience—especially because most of you who read this have had quite a bit of experience with Ignatian spirituality. I love the spirituality of Ignatius, and I want to share my experience in the hope that I can add significantly to your experience and to the ongoing evolution of that important spirituality.

I experienced my first migraine headache as I was traveling from Southern California to Los Gatos on the train, on the very day I entered Sacred Heart Novitiate in 1962. These migraine headaches lasted for fifty years and began to diminish only as I embarked on the radical transformation that I am sharing with you now. This transition not only ended my migraines, but it has had dramatic effects on every aspect of my life.

The transition began as I attended an introductory workshop given by Marshall Rosenberg, here in Portland, Oregon. Within twenty minutes of his opening remarks, I excitedly realized that the spirituality that he was talking about was really, in essence, Ignatian. This man had discovered the same thing that Ignatius had discerned about the human spirit: that desire is the most powerful force within us. I was excited. I was hooked.

I bought his book. I took classes. I attended workshops. I joined a support group. I learned everything I could about this spirituality because I could see that he had discovered the same thing that Ignatius had discovered about humanity—namely that there is a life dynamic within us that is always reaching for more life, ultimately reaching for God, the Source of Life.

I made this spirituality my own, in a way I hadn't when I was in the Society, and it changed my life.

As I became aware of the power of desire within me, my migraine headaches soon went away. I also no longer had to wear a "night guard" because of grinding my teeth at night—the grinding had stopped. My alcohol consumption dropped dramatically to about 10% of what it had been. And I also noticed that instead of frequently waking up in a troubled state, it was now very rare for me to wake up in worry.

Ignatius focused on the dynamic of desire. In almost every meditation in the Exercises, he urges us to ask for that which we desire. Ignatius hit upon this (as Bernard Lonergan put it) "inbuilt dynamism of the human spirit toward authenticity and self-transcendence." Ignatius built his spirituality on the dynamism of desire—the most powerful force in the human spirit.

Marshall Rosenberg discovered this dynamic and created a spiritual practice that embodied paying attention to the dynamism that leads us to Life. He developed a spiritual practice that starts with experiencing this dynamic within us and then allows this inner life to be the force of love and service as we progress in the world.

In my novitiate experience, the dynamic of desire was not developed. In my Long Retreat experience, the dynamic of desire was ignored. In my subsequent years in studies and teaching, the dynamic of desire never came up. In the ten years that I was in the Order, it was as if Ignatius never suggested "asking for that which you desire." It wasn't part of my spiritual formation.

What I'm sharing here describes my transition. I want to be clear; I am always in transition; I have not arrived. I still struggle with the cultural conditioning that we all struggle with, that conditioning which makes us want to act in ways that we will be safe and secure and taken care of on our own terms. And my transitioning is to live in connection with the power of desire within me—because that desire within me is the desire for Life. It is a dynamic, reaching for Life that is within all of us—reaching for the fullness of Life that Jesus proclaimed.

Joe Mitchell (California Province 1962–71) is living in Portland, Oregon, working as a mental health counselor, married to Kathy, and is gratefully beginning the most exciting phase of his wonderful life.

Nothing to Contribute

Donald R. Moses

Despite Gene Bianchi's encouragements and Don Foran's frequent and kind invitations, I have chosen not to contribute. For a simple reason: I have not had a "Spiritual Transition" à la Paul on the road to Damascus or many of our Brethren on the various roads to and from Los Gatos, Sheridan, Alma, Woodstock. Ergo, it would be silly to try to squeeze out 700 words.

I still believe in God [although the concept has changed] . . . He might be a She; happily Jesus is now a Political Zealot, not a virgin-born, resurrected, ascended fellow wrapped in the shroud of Turin; the Ghost is now a Spirit.

I still believe in Humanity [although my embrace expands almost daily . . . wife, family, adopted family, extended family, friends, classmates, teammates, Companions, American Indians, Mexican Americans, Illegal Immigrants, Sunnis, Shiites, Palestinians, Jews, Filipinos, and thanks to Gene, Vagrants.

I still believe in theological and political Liberalism, although I get more and more entrenched and committed when I see the destructiveness and blatant ignorance of Evangelicals, Conservative Catholics, TEA Party simpletons.

I still believe that teaching is the "oldest profession," although in academic life and corporate life, and whatever the subject (Philosophy, Latin, Business Conduct Guidelines, Leadership). . . . I always kept the same three mentors, Socrates, Sisyphus, Dr. Seuss.

I still believe that good team basketball is the epitome of sport [see USF of the '50s, Celtics of '60s/'70s/early '80s, UCLA of the Wooden years, Coach K's Duke program]. I see basketball as a metaphor for the other elements of my life. I love the game. I worked hard at it. However, I was a limited player—poor hands, short stubby legs, long torso—and a limited coach. [I thought teamwork, fun, everyone participating was more important than winning; players loved me, red-ass parents despised me.]

Similarly, I love God, Humanity, Liberal Thought, and Teaching. I work hard at understanding and supporting each. However, my intelligence and energy are limited.

Even if I were to try for 700 words, double-spaced, special typeface, approved font, suggested format, it would be a near impossible task. Recently, it took RRR two weeks and infinite patience to help me and Jane Mary get to a larger, more legible e-mail font. Imagine what it would take to fulfill the other Essay requirements. I end where I began. No "Spiritual Transition" yet. Maybe it's coming.

Don Moses (California Province 1959–72) and Jane Mary have one granddaughter, Christine, and a great-grandson, Joseph Otto. He retired from a career in organizational development and internal consulting with Rolm / IBM / Siemens. On his five-acre spread he has many animals: a horse, goats, dogs, cats. He recently taught Latin at Santa Catalina High School in Monterey, California and does daily tutoring for his second-grader bilingual neighbor.

The CUA DMin Game Changer

John P. Mossi, SJ

Reflecting over my sixty-nine-year pilgrim journey, of which fifty-one have been as a Jesuit, there have been many ESPN SportsCenter Game Changer events; e.g., entering Los Gatos in 1962, Vows, Ordination, meaningful friendships, important mentors, and countless significant experiences along the way. Or, would it be more accurate to use the image of a roller coaster ride? I list a number of Game Changers because whether one is a Jesuit or a Compañero, it is essential to reinvent oneself as the road alters, twists, and turns. It is easy to become stuck as those on the freeway zoom by. What perhaps worked effectively during one season of the journey might need to be jettisoned for something new, more integral and challenging at a different point in time and situation.

After spending five years in parish ministry at Our Lady of Sorrows in Santa Barbara from 1974 to 1980, with a one-year Tertianship in Wales, I transferred to the El Retiro retreat center in Los Altos. Especially during one-on-one sessions, I began asking, "Am I helping people, just spinning wheels with them, or maybe even doing harm?" I felt a need for ministry supervision, updating in theology, basic counseling skills, plus exposure to spiritualities other than Ignatian. I began a process of hunting for different types of programs from doctoral to pastoral, and eventually came across the Doctor of Ministry degree program at the Catholic University of America in DC. The DMin was an integrating blend of theology, models, methods, and praxis.

In 1982, nine years after ordination and with a backpack of personal and theological questions, I arrived at Leonard Neale House near Dupont Circle in DC. I lived with the members of the Jesuit Conference and was their token grad student. As a Californian lost in the East Coast maze of different customs and attitudes, a whole new world opened up for me. CUA was exciting with Charles Curran and Elizabeth Johnson as outstanding professors. But it was the overall academic rigor and personal stretching that the DMin offered that became my critical game changer. Slowly, I was beginning to think differently, write precisely, and open myself to group dynamics and supervision. I spent more time rewriting and editing my thesis proposal than any other document either prior or after. There were times I seriously questioned whether I was going to be able to complete the program or even if it was worth it. Was I rowing my little boat too far out into the Atlantic?

I have to say that the completion of the DMin has been my mid-life Game Changer big ticket. It provided me with the credential to enter the academic teaching club. In 1991, I became a member of the Religious Studies Department at Gonzaga University. Another new world opened up. I loved teaching, the Northwest, Hayden Lake villa, and, of course, Zags basketball. Over a period of sixteen years, I taught classes in Catholicism, Christian Spirituality, and Introduction to Pastoral Counseling. The real name of the latter course was "Everything I needed to know in Clinical Pastoral Education but was never told." I gladly gave away the listening and counseling secrets so that future ministers of diverse traditions could be theologically competent and pastorally skilled. The CUA DMin Game Changer became a vehicle to empower others on their ministerial journey.

John Mossi, SJ, (California Province 1962) currently serves in the California Province Advancement Office at Los Gatos as Associate Director for Benefactor Relations. John has attended the Compañeros retreat-for-renewal from 2011 to 2013, and plans to attend again in 2015.

Stumbling on My Journey

Dennis K. Mulvihill

Even though I did not participate in submitting something in writing, I do realize what a gift it was for each of us to reflect on the matter. What really stopped me was the lack of confidence that I had anything worthwhile to offer, much less the ability to even write about and submit it to my peer group. By the time my life in the Society was up, I had lost who I was, where I was going, much less how to get there. While teaching I came to the realization that I was seeing my life through eyes other than my own. The voices I spoke were not mine either, but those of the form-fitters who had directed me over the years. I still catch myself seeing with other people's eyes and speaking in another's voice. It was not until I started to try and stand outside myself, when I began to discover my own voice and set of eyes, that my world changed. I have stumbled a lot and will continue stumbling on my journey. Where the journey ends for me is not as important as the fact that I am more aware of being a subject rather than an object. Over the years at our reunions, and on the listserv, many of the writings and thoughts of the Companions have been a help to me on my journey. I have received many blessings and graces during the years post the Society. I am looking forward to reading what has been submitted.

Dennis Mulvihill (California Province 1959–67) lives with his wife Thelma in San Jose, California. Dennis is an inveterate reader and questioner—interested in history and in many political and theological topics. He is currently wrestling with the challenges of retirement.

Lynn George Muth, RIP July 17, 2011

Lynn & Heidi Muth

Before I joined the Society, I admit I had developed a certain emotional detachment from people, and an unreal sense of duty and hard work. I would bury angry feelings, which would then explode—leading me to fear confrontation and to repress my own anger. I worked hard to pacify the persons who were angry with me the same way that my father handled anger.

My self-esteem became tied in with intellectual achievement, yet my shyness hampered my ability to really enjoy it. This fostered a sense of restraint, a fear of making a mistake, which resulted in just maintaining my living space in a state of "organized chaos, with a lot of irons in the fire." For me this created a sense of being GOOD. With all of this said, after a year of college at Loyola University in Los Angeles, I entered the Society of Jesus in 1967.

I fell in love with St. Ignatius Loyola's "Prayer For Generosity." This prayer that starts with remembering God's gifts and love for me led me to a greater peace/union with the Trinity, with myself, my partners and with the world. As a result, the prayer was quite formative in developing my spirituality and giving me a strong spirit of generosity. In the Society I found success and power in intellectual pursuits that I then tended to live "in my head" as much as possible. I felt safe in a group like the Jesuits, which puts a high premium on intellectual ministry. This kind of life made it easy to stay "heady," yet it also made it difficult for me to relate to others unless I could serve them in some way.

I passed up many of the graces God sent my way for getting close to the Society of Jesus and people

Lynn George Muth, RIP July 17, 2011

within it. The longer I stayed as a Jesuit the more aware I became of my loneliness and difficulty in relating more than superficially with my peers. But at the same time there was a sense of God's presence and providential care throughout my time as a Jesuit. I left the Society after twelve years, just before being ordained. I just fell out of love with the Jesuits—although I still admire and respect them greatly.

My finding and connecting with the Compañeros, especially in our yearly weekend reunion, helped me straighten out my emotional difficulties and life. There I felt blessed with more self-confidence and the comfort of many friends who like me for myself, creating within me feelings of awe and peace in Church. God's love and God's will as a loving creator continued to create me, guide me, and shape me. It was sharing my struggles with the Compañeros that ultimately made me more of a whole person. This embracement of love gave me the ability to talk about my doubts and disappointments more easily. God had never abandoned me.

When the Compañeros group eventually opened the get-togethers to include spouses and partners, I was able to share my doubts, confusions, and fears with Heidi. I learned to cry more easily and feel deeper compassion for others who had their own pain. God used this healing experience within me to take care of the hurt and depression that hovered in me for years.

My eyes were then opened to Heidi's warmth and sense of humor, which helped heal my self-doubts and self-hatred. She stated that sharing the weekend with me opened her eyes to a side of me I had kept hidden. The two of us have many similar interests: we are both teachers, church musicians, good organizers, and are spiritually inclined. Her acceptance of my sexual feelings and awkwardness after the weekends has also been very healing for me. I truly marvel at her spirituality and her wonderfully unselfish attitude towards me.

Lynn Muth (California Province 1967–80) served for several years as president of West Coast Compañeros, Inc. (WCCI) and as a member of the board of directors both for WCCI and for the Loyola Institute of Spirituality. His prayer for generosity was generously answered, as his adopted children, many friends, and others on the receiving end of his love and charity will testify. He died in 2011 after a long struggle with brain cancer. Lynn composed this mini-memoir in the last months of his life with a little help from his wife Heidi.

The Eighth Sacrament

Richard C. Pfaff

Very few Catholics have done (or can do) this: receive all seven of the Church's sacraments (Baptism, Confirmation, Penance or Reconciliation, Eucharist, Matrimony, Ordination, and the Anointing of the Sick). Normally the priestly and married lives are seen as mutually exclusive. I have now received all seven. But is there another one?

I was just seventeen years old when I made the tumultuous and emotionally confusing decision to join the Jesuits. There was no lightning bolt from heaven, no peaceful prayer or apparition. Just the opposite. My life was in turmoil, turned upside down by a series of unforeseen and unpredictable events.

I was the second child born into a large Catholic family (eight children). Life in those days was much slower, and religion played an incredibly paramount role. In fact, it was the most important part of our daily existence. I frequently received the Sacrament of Eucharist, strived to be the perfect altar boy. Unfortunately in those days, sin, hell, and great gobs of guilt were equal partners with love, family fun, and inner security.

I was a typical naïve/innocent child of the 1940s. But that life was shattered in the seventh grade when a new student suddenly and unexpectedly introduced me to the "facts of life." I was totally traumatized and suddenly everything became sexual. My parents never gave me the "birds and bees" talk, and, with advancing puberty, I felt awash in a sea of sexual feelings and images. Adding to the emotional upheaval was the constant drumbeat that any single impure thought or deed was a mortal sin, damning one's soul to hell for all eternity. Girls, even my sisters, were no longer just

The Eighth Sacrament

siblings or friends but now sexual attractions. Any sexual thoughts or pleasure had to be resisted; if not, frequent confession and the Sacrament of Penance were the only means of returning to a state of grace.

High school years at a Jesuit prep school only accelerated my inner turmoil. Besides the growing attractiveness of girls, there was now for the first time (beginning in my sophomore year) dating, driving, and introduction to alcohol, especially large quantities of beer. Life on the surface was lots of fun: parties, dances, athletic events. . . . Even certain teachers, academic subjects, and various school activities excited me. I was elected class president, and in my junior year I made the varsity football team and received my Block B sweater. I was now a "big man on campus," dating a pretty girl from the all-Catholic girl's high school, drag racing my grandfather's 1937 LaSalle, drinking beer on the weekends and generally being obnoxious at the Saturday night dances in a nearby parish hall. Needless to say, my grades began taking a real nosedive.

This dissolute pattern worsened in my senior year. I was in excellent physical shape for the football season and our outstanding team gained additional notoriety due to Bing Crosby's twin boys on the roster. To my surprise, I was elected captain and later selected to every all-star football team, including All American—the first California player ever chosen.

I had no idea how to handle such honors, and my head swelled up big time! But inside, I knew I was just a naïve, undeserving kid. I began to act out the part of being a big shot. I drank more and became more sexually aggressive, although intercourse was off limits in this pre-birth control era.

Family, friends, teachers, almost everyone, wanted to know where I was going to college, what career I'd choose. I had no idea! I knew I didn't want to be a doctor like my dad. The only alternative that looked somewhat attractive was teaching. I was impressed by the young Jesuit scholastics, their rapport with the students, their community joy and obvious commitment to the Catholic faith.

One of my friends, a big lineman, was applying to the Jesuits, and this provided more comfort and motivation. In addition, a couple of the school's previous star athletes had entered the order. I visited them at the Sacred Heart Novitiate and theirs seemed like a great way of life. Besides, it gave me an "out" from the two-fold tension of my "sinful" life as well as questions about which college I'd attend. Joining the Jesuits seemed the perfect compromise. I could always leave if it didn't work out. After all, I was only seventeen.

But first, like all candidates for the Jesuits, I had to be interviewed and approved by an appointed Jesuit priest. One of the questions dealt with purity, specifically masturbation. Had I been chaste for the previous six months? A negative answer would have dashed all hope.

I lied and said yes.

No one could believe that I was giving up college, football, girls, family, and close friends for a celibate life.

On an overcast afternoon on that August 14 in 1952, I joined twenty-five other young men at the Sacred Heart Novitiate in Los Gatos. After brief introductions, we were assigned to our individual small cubicles with a simple bed, washbowl, and desk. All prized possessions were left at the gate. We were being stripped of our individuality. After a short probationary period, we would be issued a black cassock and cincture.

Supper on that first evening, eaten in silence, was soup and some vegetables. I imagined this would be my main meal for many years. But the next day, the Feast of the Assumption, the second-year novices pronounced their first vows of poverty, chastity, and obedience. It was an impressive ceremony. The entire Mass and music, especially the *Suscipe*, were an emotional roller coaster. But the real mind blower for me was the incredible feast that followed: seven courses, excellent cuisine, wines, and lively conversation.

The contrast and contradiction between these first two days haunted me for the next seventeen years. What was the Jesuit meaning of poverty? We had nothing but we were not poor. In spite of our vow, we had access to every middle-class material comfort.

Another troubling aspect of these first vows was that they were "permanent" vows—not temporary like other Orders, which had vow renewal ceremonies. In other words, there was no looking back, no backing out—these vows were for life! Was I ready for such a "marriage" at nineteen?

During these first two ascetical years, I was still guilt-ridden over my lie in the application process. I knew I had to confess it, even if it meant expulsion from the Order. I finally summoned the courage to tell our Master of Novices and then the Jesuit Provincial. Both assured me that it was the future that was now important. Needless to say, I was greatly relieved and tried to be an even more fervent novice. But should I take those first permanent vows?

Surprising to me was the almost non-existence of any sexual temptation. I had one "wet dream" in those two years, which again I fearfully confessed to the Master. It was only later that I realized my purity was an environmental chastity; i.e., with no radio, television, secular books or magazines, no contact with females or previous friends, and being surrounded only by pictures of saints, daily Mass and exhortations, spiritual readings, retreats, hours of prayer and meditation, there was really no "occasion of sin" nor much opportunity for impure thoughts.

Richard C. Pfaff

Despite my doubts, I professed my permanent vows in 1954. I was in for life. Two years of liberal studies followed by three years of philosophy went pretty quickly and uneventfully. The next three years, called regency, took place at an all-boys high school in Phoenix, where I taught Latin and English and coached football, basketball, and baseball. It was the best experience so far but the big test was on the horizon—theology and ordination in three years.

Alma College was nestled in the green foothills of Los Gatos. But my inner turmoil didn't match the outward serenity. Seemingly out of the blue, Pope John XXIII called for Vatican II. Suddenly everything was being questioned: the nature of the Church, role of the laity, priestly celibacy, birth control, freedom of conscience and on and on. Guitars replaced organs; contemporary dress replaced clerical garb. There was more freedom to interact with the opposite sex, and individual decision-making trumped blind obedience. It was a heady wine!

Again my inner clock was wound tight. Although some colleagues over the years had been released from their first "permanent" vows, I viewed Ordination as a final sentence. "Thou art a priest forever. . ." was a favorite quote. I admitted my hesitation to my spiritual director. He recommended I also seek outside psychological counseling. While helpful in understanding my relationship with my father, this did not answer my most pressing question.

Consequently, with serious inner reservations, in 1965 I went ahead with the Sacrament of Ordination. How could I turn back now?

My whole life was a paradox. Outwardly successful, a good teacher, preacher, and counselor, but inwardly I felt a constant negative refrain and increasing loneliness.

Celibacy was rapidly becoming a problem as I found myself "falling in love" with every attractive lady. Some priests, emboldened by the Church's new direction, had resigned and entered the married state. Three years after Ordination, I volunteered for Africa, hoping that distance would finally dispel my doubts. Six months later I returned and petitioned for laicization. Because I had a history of being open with my confessors, the Jesuit provincial requested Rome that I be freed from all vows, including the priesthood with the right to marry in the Church. After all these years, I felt like a free man!

One of the ladies I had met after Ordination was a young college graduate with incredible spiritual gifts and insight. She could read my inner struggle and encouraged me to face my fears and be myself. While I was still a Jesuit, we had fallen in love, exchanged kisses and hugs. In 1971 we were married in the Catholic Church.

Sadly after seventeen years of marriage and four beautiful children, we parted ways and our vows were subsequently annulled. Being self-centered and trying to start a new career, I was both ignorant of and insensitive to her needs. I had so much more to learn about women and life. I had now received all seven sacraments but was still searching for lasting love, peace, and purpose.

Even though I had left the Jesuits and then divorced, I had never left the Catholic Church. I continued to attend Mass and volunteer for various parish activities. In 1990, while attending a parish program for separated, divorced, and widowed Catholics, I fell in love with an incredibly striking woman who also had four children. We married in 1996. I now continue to learn the daily lessons of giving and receiving love, the eighth sacrament.

Dick Pfaff (California Province 1952–68) and his wife Donna live in San Jose, California, where he remains active in his parish.

Not a Tame Lion

Robert R. Rahl

Thanks to a year at Santa Clara University before entering the Society, and a heavy academic load during two years of studies in the juniorate, I had accumulated enough units to graduate from Gonzaga University in May 1968 after only a year studying philosophy at Mount St. Michael's in Spokane, Washington. I moved to Bea House on the G. U. campus to live with other Jesuit scholastics in graduate studies. While working on my philosophy MA, I taught one philosophy course each semester for three semesters. With that degree in hand in January 1970, I taught full-time in the philosophy department for the spring semester. Miraculously, that teaching experience, which I thoroughly loved, was counted as my entire regency, and I was assigned to begin theological studies in Canada in the fall at Regis College, then located in the Willowdale neighborhood of Toronto.

I left my footlocker and other odds and ends at Bea House while I attended summer theology classes at the University of San Francisco, planning to swing through Spokane and pick them up at the end of summer on my way to Toronto. During the summer, Providence—or Fate—intervened in the person of Fr. Ted Taheny, SJ. He collared me one day crossing the USF campus and pointed out that I had been away from California for three years and would be out of province for another four in Canada. Ted told me that there was an opening in the philosophy department and asked me if I wanted to teach at USF for a year. Who volunteers for an extra year of regency? In a key life-decision, that's exactly what I did, and everything ever after, of course, was changed. But that's another story.

At the end of summer, I drove to Spokane to fetch my belongings, and then turned around and drove back to San Francisco, an eighteen-hundred-mile round-trip. During summer school I had been staying in a room on the second floor of Xavier Hall, the Jesuit faculty residence at USF. The view from that room was to the east, overlooking the campus and, in the distance, the high-rises of downtown San Francisco, but for the coming year I was scheduled to move across the hall to Room 206 with its panoramic view to the west, down Golden Gate Avenue and the sparkling Richmond district, all the way to the blue Pacific, framed by Golden Gate Park on the left and the Golden Gate Bridge on the right. The room's previous occupant was Ray Leonardini, a scholastic who had left the Society just a few days before. I was supposed to move in on the following morning, but Paul Steidlmayer had somehow obtained the key ahead of time and helped me move my stuff into my new room the night before. All that Ray had left behind was a threadbare cassock, which I transferred to my old room as Paul and I schlepped all my earthly possessions across the hall. Courtesy of the vow of poverty, Jesuit scholastics are not supposed to have a lot of earthly possessions, but they *are* allowed the use of a few clothes and the books and notes necessary for studies and teaching. By midnight these items were all in place, neatly organized on the shelves and in the closet of my spartan new quarters. All was ready to take up my official residency the next day. That night I slept in my old room.

In the morning I got up and went across the hall to Room 206. I opened the door with my new key and did the mother of all double takes. The room was completely empty. I double-checked the room number. Yup, 206. In a disoriented daze I went down the hall to see Father Minister, Tommy O'Rourke, SJ. I reported what had happened. He told me that I should check with Mr. Muscat, a Maltese layman who served as handyman and general factotum. He had a cubbyhole office in the basement.

Mr. Muscat had been assigned to clean out Ray's room that morning. Surprised at the quantity and quality of what had been "left behind," Mr. Muscat went back to Fr. O'Rourke and asked him what he should do with all of it. Without checking the room for himself—it *was* all of two doors down the hall—Fr. Minister gave the order: "Burn it! Burn it all!"

By the time I found Mr. Muscat, he was dutifully shoveling my books, clothes, and years of class notes into the furnace. It made a cheerful blaze. I stopped him before he was actually able to "Burn it all," but there was one irreplaceable item that was lost forever. Mary Waldron, a woman on the theology faculty at Gonzaga, and a fellow fan of the *Chronicles of Narnia* by C. S. Lewis, had painted a large, beautiful watercolor of a golden lion for me as a going-away present. It depicted the scene in *The Lion, the Witch, and the Wardrobe* where Beaver tells Lucy about Aslan, the lion who is the King of that world, a Lord who is full of surprises.

> "Safe?" said Mr. Beaver; "don't you hear what Mrs. Beaver tells you? Who said anything about safe? 'Course he isn't safe. But he's good. He's the King, I tell you. . . . He's wild, you know. Not like a tame lion."

Not a tame lion—not tame at all. I moved my surviving earthly goods back to Room 206. The golden lion had gone up in flames, but the Golden Gate was still there, shining in the mid-morning sun, and at least I still had something to wear: Ray Leonardini's cassock.

Robert Rahl was in the California Province from 1963 to 1973. In the course of time, he retired from two careers, first as a professor and dean of humanities, and later as a chief information officer and director of information technology services. He found life after retirement helping to facilitate online communications for his fellow Compañeros. He is finishing a three-year term serving as WCCI president.

A New Language

James W. Riley

In childhood my first conversion came at Christmas with a sudden awareness upon seeing my parents enjoy the children opening presents. Giving felt better than receiving. My adolescent turning point at Seattle Prep was the consciousness of the joy in study and learning. My transformations of adulthood were the decision to become a Jesuit and, in mature years, using the same discernment method, to leave celibate institutional living. I chose to enter family life, and I had the opportunity to work in a back-to-the-land spiritual community developing new images, symbols, and rituals that expressed the radical cultural shift of our times. In my senior years, a turning point entailed learning to survive the loss of a love when my wife of twenty-eight years went to her high school reunion and never returned.

If I think of my fingers as representing five stages of my life, at seventy-seven I am on the little finger and can see how many changes at different stages turn on a single point like the formation of a droplet of rain around the nucleus of an ice crystal. On my thumb I vividly recall Christmas morning as a boy of ten drawing back from the commotion of opening presents, amazed by the joy I could see in my parents eyes. I began experimenting by giving gifts on birthdays and other occasions of sibling triumphs and noticing how it made me and others feel.

On my index finger I recall as a fifteen-year-old discovering the joy of learning, especially learning to read by asking the "right questions": what is he saying, what does he mean, is it true, and so what? My adolescence was an impacted turning point under the influence of my Jesuit debate coach. I felt the passion of asking and answering questions as a way to do good. I became valedictorian of my class and, at twenty-one, gave away everything I owned, said good-bye to my girlfriend and put on a black robe.

On my middle finger I see my vows at Sheridan turned me towards becoming a priest serving God in an intellectual tradition as a teacher. Learning a method of discerning the spirit was a turning point in my life. The ascetic seminary life encouraged me to live more in my head than in my body, ungrounded in place or passion.

On my ring finger my island life revolved around family, community, and place. We lived in a small town facing the North Cascade mountains, where it seemed under any rock you might find another artist or natural mystic. My wife and I raised three children in an old farmhouse located half way between the Catholic church and the funeral home. My vows transformed themselves into family life. Instead of a "poverty" of wealth there were bills to be paid, instead of "chastity" there was pure sacramental loving, instead of "obedience" there was family. Delivering the US mail by day and teaching at night, we raised three kids who are on their own, and now I live alone.

The loss of a love was the turning point on my little finger. The sudden emptiness was unspeakable but then came the awareness of new possibilities, of the opportunity to become a new person and the surprising joy of divorce. I adopted the George Costanza philosophy of "doing the opposite" and looked at every action through my day from diet to exercise to community involvement and began to make changes in my habits. Surviving the loss of a love has become a thriving of love in my life.

Jim Riley (Oregon Province 1957–84) is continuing his transformations in or around Chinook Learning Community on Whidbey Island. He remains inspired by the late eco-theologian Thomas Berry, after whom the main meeting hall at Chinook is named.

As Time Moves On
Still a Companion of Jesus

Antonio Salcido

Let me start as David Copperfield did by tracing my life back to my childhood, which was filled with so many wonders and wonderful angels, among them my saintly grandmothers and my double-dare-me saintly Aunt Maria. When I think of them I am brought to those tears that Ignatius mentions in his Spiritual Exercises.

It is no wonder that I chose the way of St. Ignatius and the Jesuits. As a child, I was always comfortably embraced by a Jesuit environment. El Paso had been stamped with the Jesuit missionary spirit many years before I was born. St. Ignatius was my grandparents' parish church, and I attended many Masses there, went to some catechism classes, served as the godchild of a graduating class of the school, and even served as an altar boy at one time. Then I went to Guardian Angel School, which was attached to Guardian Angel Church, again a church founded by the early Italian and Spanish Jesuit missionaries in this area of the Southwest.

I have often wondered why I did not join the Claretians because, as an elementary school student at Guardian Angel, I served as an altar boy with such zeal for many years that at times I left the house without breakfast just to serve the Mass of my great friend, Padre Labrador, a Claretian priest from Spain. And to make my connections with the Jesuits or the priests even tighter, my Aunt Maria, the saint I mentioned earlier, worked at the priests' residence as cook and *spiritual director*. (That last title I have given her without any hesitation because I am certain she gave more spiritual light to the priests than she received from them.)

One thread that connects me in elementary school with the Jesuits is a bus ride—yes, at my age at almost three quarters of a century I can still vaguely contemplate that scene—with my best friend, Herman, who was a fellow altar boy at Guardian Angel, and whose brother was a Jesuit in the Mexican Province. At this time he started telling me stories of his brother's adventures and the wonders of his studies during his Jesuit formation years. At this same time I also read of the Jesuit spirit of missionaries like Isaac Jogues and his Companions, who had brought the message of Christ to the New World.

Now add a new ingredient to the child in growth: my grandmother dreamed of a priest in the family. The story is that one of her sons had wanted to be a priest but somehow he met his future wife in the neighborhood. But her dream continued to another level: one of her grandchildren had to be a priest!

Now we jump up to my time in high school when I spoke with the Christian Brother Alphonsus, the principal, who was interviewing all the seniors about their future goals. I told him that I maybe was interested in becoming a priest, and that I also wanted to work with young people. That's when he mentioned the Jesuits.

One year out of high school, I still was not certain what road to take. So after having thought about my nebulous future, I decided to talk to a Jesuit who was a good friend of my mother. He referred me to other Jesuits and after all the interviews I set off to Grand Coteau, the Jesuit novitiate of the Southern (New Orleans) Province.

When I was on the train for the day-long journey, I felt like I would never see my parents or friends again. Of course, things did not prove to be so dire.

Antonio Salcido

Grand Coteau, Louisiana, is forever etched in my mind. I believe that God placed this patch of earthly paradise between swamps and oak trees showered with Spanish moss. The warm hospitality of the Cajun people and other idyllic jewels of Evangeline Country immediately captured my soul. What a gift from the Creator for those of us in those four Jesuit formative years.

After novitiate and juniorate in Grand Coteau, we boarded a bus and traveled to Mobile, Alabama, to begin the three years of Philosophical Studies and other undergraduate work at the Jesuit House of Studies on the Spring Hill College campus. And to influence my formative years, these were the times of the Civil Rights movement which was sprouting there in the South, not too far from Mobile! The times, they really were a-changing, as Bob Dylan sang during those turbulent years.

After those formative years, I was off to Brazil as a Jesuit Missionary to Campinas, São Paulo. There, as a Jesuit Scholastic, I worked at a Community Development Center, Centro Social Presidente Kennedy, for about two years and then was sent to Theological Studies in São Leopoldo, Rio Grande do Sul. And it was there after a half a year of studies and during the yearly eight-day retreat that Jesuits make, that I saw clearly that Christ had chosen another path for me, one where I could still serve him as a Companion of Jesus and as a member of his Church.

Now the question pops up: What made you decide to leave the Society of Jesus? After my eight-day retreat and prayerful discernment during my first year of theology, I wanted to confirm my decision to follow Christ by another path. I spoke with Father Geza, SJ my spiritual director, who supported my decision to leave the Society.

Brazil opened my eyes and heart in such ways that I now saw the Church and the following of Christ with different insights and dimensions. The Church in the late 1960s had also opened up its closed doors and new lights began illuminating—I'm certain the Holy Spirit was there—those dark quarters that had kept the faithful in medieval theologies that enslaved the faithful with sin, guilt, and other burdens. And I really think that Christ had given me this great opportunity to be His Companion in His Company for those years so that I could share what I had learned in the Jesuits with those whom I would meet thereafter.

I have nothing but admiration for the ideals of St. Ignatius of Loyola, even though there are some dimensions of the Society of Jesus that I pray will change and undergo a substantive renovation; after all, aren't we all sincerely praying that the new young Jesuits will set their world on fire not only in the twenty-first century, but always *Ad Majorem Dei Gloriam*?

Tony Salcido (New Orleans Province 1958–67) was an educator and administrator for many years with the LAUSD and retired in 2002. He is happily married to Maria-José Chiavoloni Salcido and they have a daughter, Sandra Christina, and a son, Jason Paul. They live in Thousand Oaks, California, and are involved with helping the needy at their local parish through the St. Vincent de Paul Society and often go to Brazil to support the Jesuit missionaries and the Dispensario Imaculada that provides poor families with basic necessities.

Jiao

Michael R. Saso

I entered the novitiate in Los Gatos, California, in 1948, and some of my most memorable moments in my early years took place at Mount St. Michael's in Spokane, Washington, where the camaraderie of fellow California and Oregon Jesuits—cherished forever—took place. I later worked on the Spokane, Kalispell, Coeur d'Alene, and Blackfoot/Piegan reservations. I asked to transfer to the Oregon Province, to serve the Blackfoot people; the answer from Rome was: "Take the next boat to China."

I sailed to Taiwan on the *Sally Maersk* on July 31, 1955; two typhoons and three ports later (Iloilo, Cebu, Manila), I arrived in Jilong harbor, Taiwan. No Jesuits were there to meet me, but Bro. Bob Griffin, SJ, in mid-afternoon drove us (Tony Gandolfo, SJ, an Argentinian, and I) to Hsinchu, Taiwan, where we were greeted with the words, "Why did you come? We thought it would be Dave McWhirter or Ed Malatesta." (I worked much of my life to help close friend Ed Malatesta, SJ, come to China, which he did in 1992; RIP, 1999!)

The words we learned in Chinese expressed the beauty of Hsinchu County, Guanxi village, nestled against the 12,000 foot high hills of Taiwan.

I moved from this peaceful Hakka village to Hsinchu City, in December 1955; a Daoist festival, called Jiao 醮 ("offering") welcomed us! My doctoral dissertation, *Daoism & the Rite of Cosmic Renewal,* was published in 1972 by Washington State University Press. The Daoists of Hsinchu remain close to my heart.

From 1958–62 in the Philippines, I pursued theology studies on mile-high Mount Mirador, in

Baguio City. This venue provided a stunning view of Lingayen peninsula and Bolinao point to the west. Stars in the sky melded with the lights of fishing boats in the Lingayen Gulf at night. The China mainland, 180 miles over the horizon, at last allowed entrance to practice there, with Daoists, in 1986.

"Why did you come to China?" our Chinese classmates in Baguio asked me. "We do not want any foreigners, insensitive to our feelings, culture, or spirituality, in China." We became close friends, after that! I asked why they told their true feelings to me. Their response: "Because we know you will never be made Jesuit superior!" Buddhist & Daoist practices learned in Taiwan did not sit well with our Austrian, Spanish, and French professors!

After Tertianship, I asked to work in a parish in Taiwan. Fr. Onate ordered me, "under Holy Obedience," to study classical Chinese and language-teaching methods instead. I asked why. He replied, "Because you understood your Chinese classmates." "They do not at all agree!" I assured him. "You are then assigned to teach language and culture to foreigners, at Fu Jen University."

PhD studies in Classical Chinese require fluent Japanese. The best profs were at Kyoto University in Japan. I went there to study from 1965–67, and literally fell in love with Japan; I return every year, *"to spring cherry blossoms, summer iris, fall maple leaves, winter plum flowers in the snow."*

London University invited me to do my doctoral dissertation, with a full scholarship, 1967–69; my PhD was awarded in 1970.

For decades I studied and wrote on Daoism & Chinese culture and Tantric Buddhism; I published fourteen books in English, a twenty-five volume supplement to the Daoist Canon in Chinese, and a Japanese-Chinese study on Daoist legerdemain taught

Michael R. Saso

and preserved by Daoist Masters in Taiwan, and the Daoist Mountains of China.

The most amazing of all life experiences, by far, was the study of Daoism, (see *Daoist Master Zhuang*, third edition, 2012). Videos showing Master Zhuang's teachings can be seen on YouTube and http://www.michaelsaso.org. The teachings of Master Zhuang, the Tendai Tantric Buddhist of Kyoto (*Tendai Tantric Ritual*, University of Hawaii Press; YouTube, *The Agni-Hotra Fire Rite*), & Tantric Buddhism of Tibet, are analogous!

I left the Jesuits in 1968 to marry, and was given a rescript to celebrate Mass "*dum episcopum benevolum eum accipere inveniri potest.*" I married Nariko Akimoto (deceased), and we had two daughters, Theresa and Mari; two granddaughters, Cyren, Pelé. I have practiced Daoist and Buddhist meditation until the present day. I taught religion at University of Hawai'i, Manoa Campus, 1974–90, and from 1990 to the present I work and teach in China, Tibet, and Kyoto, Japan. In 1997 I was re-incardinated to the priesthood in the Diocese of San Jose; I was assigned to St Angela parish, Monterey Diocese, to care for my aging mother who passed away in 2004.

Life is to be cherished, I feel deeply, because of our camaraderie as Compañeras/Compañeros. I am honored to be a member. I enjoy bringing Compañeros with me to Tibet, Beijing, and Kyoto! My deepest gratitude: one family, united in empathy and close friendship!

Michael Saso was in the California Province from 1948 to 1968. In addition to the rich array of biographical information in Michael's narrative, he built five schools in north Tibet (Qinghai), Yunnan, Kham province, and Lhasa; one school for girls in Faizalbal, Afghanistan; Daoist Studies Center in Beijing; a five-thousand book library in Los Angeles, California, focused on Comparative Spirituality studies.

Chips and Slivers
A Poem for Maureen

F. Joseph Schneider

Chips and slivers
Piled high in corners,
Dust of each day's labor
Blanketing the room,
Quiet evidence of uncounted days
Molding, carving, coaxing out
The hidden form that is the
Sculptor's art.
In space quite different
We too, with instruments
More delicate than sculptor's
Chisel, labor to create, to
Shape, to fashion bonds of
Steady faith and equal trust,
To bring about the hidden
Form that is the best of us.
The effort is not in vain,
And as a marble that holds out
Against the vagaries of time,
Our union will endure against the blast
And like a David meet the years steadfast,
Confident the work is strong—that
Constancy and gentle nurture
Yield their grace.

Joe Schneider was in the Oregon Province novitiate (1961-63), then left to study in Seattle University's Honors Program where he met his future wife, Maureen. He taught English for twenty-six years at Gonzaga Prep and relishes retirement, especially family gatherings with their two sons and much-loved grandchildren.

Shedding Skin

Gary R. Schouborg

Leaving the Jesuits in spring 1970 felt inevitable and natural, like a snake shedding its outgrown skin. There was no drama, no spiritual turmoil, no conflicted feelings. There was only a peaceful sense of release from a tomb whose subtly stifling presence I had not previously noticed.

This sense of continuity flowed from years of philosophical reflection, which had moved me to become a Jesuit after graduating from Loyola University of Los Angeles in 1958. Thanks to Jesuit education and Vatican II, I gradually shed an otherwordly orientation toward the next life for a this-worldly emphasis on this one. Eventually, that process led me to realize, like Molière's bourgeois gentleman who realized that he had been speaking prose all his life, that secular humanism was my natural language.

My move to the empirical—taking this life as more than boot camp for the next one—inevitably included sex. Still at an emotional remove from something that personally involving, I tiptoed into it by questioning how I could counsel human beings when I was not emotionally involved with the female half of them. Inevitably, my perspective became more concrete when I taught philosophy at the all-male Loyola University, 1964–1966. In socially interacting with students and their girlfriends, I was chagrined to find that, although I had developed a kind of intellectual sophistication, I was as emotionally underdeveloped as I had been in 1958 when I "left the world" for the Jesuit novitiate in Los Gatos, California.

I joined the Jesuits primarily for two reasons: to bring to the world the good news of natural law theory—that God's laws are not tests to qualify for heaven, but a kind of instruction manual for humans to flourish; and to explore inner space, as I have always thought of the spiritual path. Secondarily, I found two benefits to balance the costs of celibacy: to simplify my moral life by paying off seemingly endless smaller moral debts with one big sacrifice; and to deal with my grotesque insecurity in the battle of the sexes by surrendering.

My Jesuit years helped me to begin standing on my own two feet intellectually and spiritually. But that very development also made it painfuly clear that I was nowhere near able to do so emotionally. So when I "returned to the world," I was eager to explore. However, since wisdom requires emotional development, I was still naïve not only about women but people generally. It took me years to reduce dealing with others through generalizations in favor of relating to them in their uniqueness. Of course, that is a lesson that the best of us will still be learning till our dying breath; but I had little idea then how long a road lay before me.

At the start, I assumed that my experience was like everyone else's, so that those who remained Jesuits lacked either the intellectual capacity or strength of heart to think through their lives thoroughly. Only several years later had I a sufficiently nuanced understanding of my own journey to see how at least some who remained Jesuits might have done so from strengths that I did not have.

To get to that point, I had to lay out my heart to be broken in one romantic encounter after another. A longer reflection at http://garynini.com/em-shamefaces.htm provides a theoretical framework and explanation for why I was such a slow learner. I was repeatedly disappointed because a deep and abiding shame left me misunderstanding the real causes of my rejections. There were times when I thought that I might have bitten off more life-seeking than I could chew, that perhaps I should not have jumped into relationships so nakedly without some sort of emotional parachute. But at such times, I was gratified and strengthened by a force within me that exultantly shouted out at Life: "Give me your best shot. I can take anything you can throw at me." In every such moment I felt ever more cleansed of my shame, ever more a man, ever more capable of regarding others with that respect from which emerges true affection. Only through that process was I readied to meet Nini through craigslist.com on June 27, 2007, have her move in with me on July 24, and marry her that Christmas Eve.

Gary Schouborg (California Province 1958–70) and his wife Nini live in Walnut Creek, California. He is deeply interested in Strategic and Tactical Performance Improvement.

The Night That Changed My Life

Raymond A. Schroth, SJ

When I arrived at Fordham University in the fall of 1951, I automatically signed up for R.O.T.C. That I would eventually go into the United States Army had been long understood. The Korean War was raging; so, since I would inevitably be drafted, I wanted to be an officer, and the program would take me through college before sending me abroad. Besides, the army was in my blood. My father had won the Distinguished Service Cross in World War I. He had taught my younger brother Dave and me to ride polo ponies at the 112th Field Artillery base outside Trenton, New Jersey, when we were three years old; his friends were in the American Legion, so we displayed our enormous American flag on holidays; and he had taken us to see *Sergeant York* and *Wilson* at an impressionable age.

Meanwhile the Jesuits I had admired at Saint Joseph's Prep in Philadelphia, and some whom I encountered at Fordham, were convinced I should join them, and their letters during the Fordham years kept stirring the embers of a vocation. Finally my mentor, historian Joseph R. Frese, SJ, whose Mass I served every morning except during my junior year in Paris, told me that the well-meaning recruiters had no right to push me, that if I was to join I would know when the time came.

After graduation, tensions between religious ideals and military culture surfaced at Officers' Training School at Fort Bliss, Texas. Juarez, Mexico, today famous for its mass graves of drug dealers' enemies, was then the soldiers' weekend playground, with its strip-tease bars and brothels and boys selling their sisters on the streets. I was appalled that some of my fellow student-officers seemed to have no religious principles or even intellectual curiosity; one told me that religion and politics were two subjects that no officer should discuss. Since they were the topics that most turned me on, that would leave me speechless for two years. Fortunately, I made some friends from Boston College.

I wrote to my father about this, and he replied that I should withhold judgment on my comrades: on the battlefield my life would depend on these very men. More serious was the pep talk we received where the speaker reminded us of the fundamental principle that should guide us: We are hired killers.

If I remember correctly, I wore my second lieutenant's uniform to Christmas Midnight Mass at the Trenton Cathedral in 1955, a week before I was to fly to Germany and report to the 62nd Antiaircraft Artillery Battalion in Mannheim and take responsibility for four fifty-caliber machine guns mounted in turrets on half-tracks and four forty millimeter antiaircraft guns mounted on tank bodies, all manned by a platoon of fifty men. But the future-priest bug still surfaced from time to time. I had a girlfriend whom I loved named Sally, but I was not in a strong position to pursue her. As the organ roared and the choir soared, the Bishop of Trenton began his solemn procession down the aisle. Although my journalist father told me years later that this bishop would be partly reformed by Vatican II, he was known for an almost fascist rigidity. He was overweight and, to my eyes, exuded pomposity. I offered a silent prayer that I might be attracted to the Jesuits, whose rules excluded ambition to hierarchical status.

The two years in Germany were exhilarating. On the first day, our battalion commander, a colonel, motivated the new officers with his conviction that the Russians would attack that winter. The idea that we might soon be required to kill hundreds of other young men never gelled. I believed that our cause was just, and that we had to do what was necessary. After a short term as a platoon leader the colonel brought me onto his staff as the battalion communications officer. When we pulled out of the barracks for a major, several-day training maneuver, when the Hungarian uprising seemed to offer an opportunity for those among my colleagues who needed a war, I was assigned the role of leader of the Aggressors.

In a war game, the Aggressors attack the main encampment to challenge its security. In my role as "enemy," I took this seriously and was determined to take the battalion by surprise. So in the darkest night I led my Aggressor troops silently through a German forest, undetected, to the sleeping camp and charged in. I heaved a tear gas bomb into a nearby tent. The victory was ours. But in that tent the tear gas had taken a lieutenant by surprise, and he had gone into shock.

We bundled his unconscious form into the back of a jeep and drove through the night to the nearest hospital. It was the longest drive of my life. Yes, they should have been ready for an enemy tear-gas attack, but this man was trapped in an enclosed space. I was responsible for whatever happened. Had I killed my first man? With his silent body beside me I prayed: "God, if you want me to become a Jesuit, don't let this man die."

He did not die. The next day we both went back to work. But if he had not recovered my future as either a soldier or a Jesuit would have disintegrated.

In the years ahead, as Korea was replaced by Vietnam, I realized slowly that, because of my father's background, it had never occurred to me

The Night That Changed My Life

that the United States could wage an unjust war. But during theology at Woodstock during the 1960s, influenced by the National Catholic Reporter, Commonweal, and my fellow young Jesuits, I slowly realized the time had come to be ashamed of the foreign policy of the nation I had served in uniform. Covering for *America* the anti-war demonstrations at the Democratic National Conventions in Chicago in 1968, I was tear-gassed by the Chicago police and staggered to a fountain in Grant Park to wash my eyes. Four years later I visited my family when Nixon and Kissinger were ordering the mass bombing of Hanoi. My father, then 82, a man who had tried to re-enlist after Pearl Harbor and whose patriotism had forced him to support every war, changed. I just remember him shaking his head sadly and, with a heavy sigh, saying, "All those lives."

Ray Schroth, SJ, (New York Province 1957) is literary editor of America *magazine.*

All Is Well

George Seeber

I wanted so badly to serve God, so I entered the Jesuits from Loyola High School, Los Angeles, in August of 1951. "You keep the rules, and the rules will keep you," said the Master of Novices. I did everything correctly. I was fast reaching perfection. All is well.

Fifteen years of "training": hard work at studies, discipline, meditation, cooperation, community-building. All is well.

Six years at a Jesuit high school in San Jose, California, sharing religious values with high school students, organizing retreats and adult education, being a community-builder within the community. All is well.

Five years at a Jesuit Retreat House in Los Altos, California. Directing priests and religious and laity in five-day and thirty-day retreats, offering weekend retreats to the cops and the firemen, etc. Very successful. All is well.

Age forty-five. Mid-life. The pain is getting worse. I still keep the rules, AND ... "How are you, George?" my friends would ask. When I was honest I'd say, "Most of me is fine; but part of me is crying."

The pain got more intense. The hurt permeated my being. I could not stand it. I needed relief! Where? Who? How?

Psychotherapy in 1976. Still somewhat suspicious. Problems only. Big problems, please. And big bucks too! The Jesuits paid the big bucks no questions asked. They trusted that I would do all AMDG, for the greater glory of God. And so it was, and the pain continued. I needed relief from the pain, the great motivator. For nine months the therapist asked about my family life. I grew up fine. No dominating mother; no distant father. All is well.

I had whispered to a psychiatrist ten years previously: "Maybe I am homosexual." He said, " You don't walk like one; you don't talk like one; you cannot be one." I breathed a DEEP sigh of relief. I am not one of THEM.

After all they are all alike, "those homos." They like "little boys." They are "objectively disordered and have a natural inclination to sin," says the Church to this day. Who, me? I feel very normal. All is well with me keeping the rules. I am a holy person. Who are you talking about? I'm not one of THEM.

I'll never forget the day I woke up knowing I was a member of a minority group: reviled, hated, looked-down-upon—on the same line in moral theology manuals as "bestiality." AND YET I experienced myself as VERY GOOD.

Ah, a leave of absence. Live outside the Jesuits to see where you stand regarding men and women. One month at the Esalen Institute in the Big Sur. Walk around in the nude at the baths; try massage; fall in and out of love. That should be a great teacher.

Finally, relief. Not at Esalen—while that helped—but a therapist in San Francisco who gifted me with "listening." To my feelings, to my fantasy life, to my desires. All geared to another man to love. I was homosexual.

But that terrible word and that "objective disorder," and that natural inclination to sin and evil. Who are they speaking of?

A desire to return to the Jesuits after a two years' "leave of absence"—a desire to go to a Jesuit parish in San Jose. Seven years there to feel the shame, the guilt, the doubts, the pain of being homosexual. While serving the people of God in a most loving way. Time and Holy Family parish and therapy diminished "the hurt."

Healing was on the way. Not homosexual, but rather "gay," with acceptance and love.

George Seeber (California Province 1951–91) stayed seven years at Holy Family Parish, San Jose, took one year Sabbatical, and then left the Society with tears. Today he is in a happy relationship with his partner of more than fifteen years.

The Phantom of Seattle

Jerome B. Seitz

During my glory days in high school, I was an athlete. She was a cheerleader. The night I sank three long shots in thirty seconds, she led the cheers. The night we tied the second-best football team in the state for the Columbia Basin Championship, she led more cheers. The day I hit her a home run at North Central she was ecstatic. So it went. Sock hops, proms, Knight Flights. Then came senioritis and the big slump. No college scholarship offers, except from Idaho, and nobody with self-respect in those days wanted to go to Idaho. There was a possible invitation to rookie baseball camp in Florida though.

Meanwhile, Fathers Luke Kreuzer, John Dalgity, and Joe Showalter thought that I would make a good Jesuit. "Put your money in the heaven where the moth no go," as a parishioner at Guadalupe would say years later. Beauty incorruptible, the Fathers said, awaited even in this life. Go to Sheridan. Work for God. There is no higher calling. Bob Jay, my idol from Loyola had done it. Ignatius of Loyola did it. Len Sitter had done it. If they could do it, so could I! So after a sad goodbye to my constant cheerleader girlfriend, I ventured off to the novitiate.

Seven years later, five years after first vows, I attended summer school classes at Gonzaga. Oops, there she was, the cheerleader that I had left behind, taking summer classes too. Only now she was a nun! Passing occasionally on campus, we discussed the weather, classes, the past. I don't know if she was uncomfortable, but I certainly was. Right then and there the son of Maia, Mercury, or perhaps it was Gabriel, or Raphael, appeared to me on campus reminding me, *"Vovisti paupertatem, castitatem, obedientiam perpetuam in Societate Jesu.* If your eye scandalize you pluck it out. If your ex-girlfriend walks on the same campus, get out of town."

Seattle University the following summer was ideal, the perfect place for a student, a hermit. Every day after class I went straight to my cave to study: sociology for Fr. Suvain, statistics for Fr. Gaffney. One afternoon I was summoned out of my cave by the president, Fr. Jack Fitterer. Trembling with fright about what I might have done to merit a reprimand from the president, I trudged to his office. "*Pater Magister vult te videre*," as we all remembered from the novitiate and juniorate.

The previously mentioned trembling was minor compared to the major anxieties that followed. For there was this Phantom of Delight, when first she gleamed upon my sight, that lovely apparition sent to be a moment's ornament...

"This is ex-Miss Seafair," said the president, "my secretary's daughter. She is entering the convent, and I have an old trunk that I'm giving her. I need someone to take it to her house. Would you be willing to do that for me?"

"Well, I g-u-e-s-s I could."

After that afternoon I reluctantly spent even more time in my cave. Jupiter was going to have no need to send Mercury again. These were pre-desktop computer days, so all calculations had to be painstakingly plotted on large paper—a multi-hour task. Fr Gaffney considerately offered to provide a tutor for any of us interested in learning to operate the Marchant & Frieden Business machines. Newly ordained Fr Jim Kaufer and I signed up. And there she appeared again. The Phantom ex-Miss Seafair had been appointed our tutor. Standard Deviations, Linear Regressions, Correlation Coefficients, Chi Squares never seemed so interesting. Marvelous how easy they were when you had such a tutor, and a machine to help. Jim Kaufer often absented himself to say first Masses, or visit friends. The Phantom and I, alone with the machines, talked about the weather, the

Jerome B. Seitz

classes, the past; we discussed the parades, the banquets, the trip to Kyoto, the many SU Jesuits who constantly enquired about her spiritual life. She revealed how she had come to want to be a nun, and I told her how I had decided to become a priest. Gabriel hurried the summer along and whisked her off to the convent. The press was there to chronicle her departure. I went back to my cave to study alone. "If your eye . . ."

Afterwards came Christmas cards, summer visits; our paths crossed. Several years passed. The Phantom was turning into a ghost—a pale, thin ghost. Common life was sapping her life. She, like I, had successes, yes, lots of them—studies, teaching, counseling, coaching. But something was missing in both our lives.

For me, ordination beckoned. I approached it with very mixed feelings. But what was I to do? *Paupertatem, castitatem, obedientiam perpetuam* . . . If I left the Society what would my dad say? What would happen to my immortal soul? I persevered. With great faith.

Almost at the end of that first year after Ordination, I received a letter from ex-Miss Seafair. "I hope you won't think less of me for doing this but I'm going to leave the convent!" "Heavens no," I replied. "I totally understand. I have loved you since the first day I saw you on campus, and you couldn't do anything that would change that."

These were the years right after Vatican II. Souls in conflict discussed the possibilities of change in the church: the ban on birth control might be lifted; the pope might permit a married clergy. We both picked up on that one, big time. She had a Sister Superior in her convent who had a friend in high places who said that was a high probability. I spent the summer in Seattle, she in Ellensburg, not so very far away for a weekend bus trip. She was free of vows; she wanted to get married. I wanted to wait a bit for the pope to catch up with the fast-changing world. Mercury appeared again, "*Vovisti p.c.o. perpetuam . . .*"

Upset, she moved to the Midwest for further graduate studies. Upset, I went back to work in Tacoma. Fires had been lit, though, and both of us found other relationships. Life as a nun and life as a priest were not for us, nor was waiting for a change that might never come comfortable. But she was gone.

The next time Mercury would have to visit me, I decided I would tell him I wasn't waiting for the pope to change; I had changed. After three outwardly successful, but inwardly tumultuous years, I left the Society.

The ex-cheerleader, in those topsy-turvy years in the sixties, became an ex-nun who married her ex-principal, an ex-priest. Fr Jack Fitterer, the ex-president of Seattle U. and an ex-Jesuit married an Episcopalian woman priest and became an Episcopalian priest himself.

The Sister Superior who had counseled ex-Miss Seafair about impending changes, eloped with a Jesuit classmate of mine. The Superior's deserted-friend-in-high-places, Fr Luke Kreuzer, was found dead in his office with a gun nearby. Ex-Miss Seafair, married, became a wonderful counselor and later a financial consultant, and I have been happily married for forty-two years to a lovely lady who, herself, was another apparition. Now I see with eye serene the very pulse of the machine, a being breathing thoughtful breath, a traveler between life and death, a spirit still and bright with something of angelic light.

Where have all religious gone, long time passing? It seems that many found saving immortal souls for the next life less attractive that nurturing each other and procreating souls for this life. They have transitioned.

Jerry Seitz (Oregon Province 1953–70) and his wife Victoria live in Normandy Park, Washington. He teaches Latin at Kennedy High School in Burien, where he was Academic Dean for many years, and she is a King County District Court judge. They have three grown children.

Chopsticks in Hand

Robert K. Semans

When my class in the Society went to Berkeley to begin theology studies, I took a detour and attended San Jose State University for two years to study fine art. I'd made a pretty convincing case for doing this sooner rather than later, and the provincial kindly gave me the go-ahead. At this same time I was beginning to struggle with doubts about my faith. The existence of God no longer seemed so certain. When I asked a classmate at Berkeley one day during a visit whether he ever had doubts about his faith, he looked at me in surprise (or maybe it was shock) and said emphatically "No!" I realized at that point that I was no longer marching in step.

Up until that time my whole experience of church, spirituality, Society was one of trying to live up to, to fit in and to feel part of. Now something didn't fit. I didn't quite fit.

I took a leave of absence from the Society and went to Florence to study with a well-known teacher there, while also working my second year with Gonzaga University's Junior Year Abroad program. This was a great experience. Fine program. Great Jesuits, and terrific kids . . . about 100 juniors. I continued to go to Mass and maintain some sort of spiritual life though it was no doubt anemic. I was too busy dating, having fun, painting and drawing and generally enjoying the "good life." I had discovered women and Jesus didn't stand a chance.

I no longer felt completely a part of the Jesuits (no surprise there!) though I had close friends in the Society. I was not really a true "civilian," more of a "pretend" civilian. This situation persisted for several more years because I wasn't ready to leave the Jesuits. Guilt over "turning my back on Jesus" and leaving my fellow Jesuits still had a firm grip on me. Despite my shaky adherence to the vows, I still had some residue of a conscience.

Thus I ended up at Seattle University for a year to try to work out once and for all a decision. Growing loneliness, friendly coeds and the inevitable came to pass. I left the Society in 1973. For a number of years thereafter I pursued a career in Art and discovered true poverty. I married a wonderful woman from Louisiana who had a seven-year-old daughter. So, instant family. My marriage was at Holy Family church. My dear friend Fr. Joe Spieler, SJ, was the celebrant.

My marriage got off to a rocky start and somewhere in the second year I also found myself in Alcoholics Anonymous. My wife and I still went to Sunday Mass but neither of us was truly connected. I joined AA and then things got really interesting.

Two years into sobriety, I woke up one day and any sense of the "old" God was gone as if "He" had sneaked out in the middle of the night without saying goodbye. It was a very disturbing experience. For some time I thought "He" had left because I didn't deserve to have faith. Then gradually I accepted where I was, as opposed to where I SHOULD be, and as someone advised, continued to get up each morning, put on my shoes, put one foot in front of the other and kept an open mind. My AA friends had all found a Higher Power and mine had left town with no forwarding address. Now I didn't fit into AA either. I was a pretend recovering Alky because I didn't have a Higher Power. I was a fraud.

About this time I ran into Br. Tom Marshall, SJ, up at the novitiate, and he invited me to participate in a meditation group he had each Thursday evening. This was a life changing experience because I began to pay attention to what was going on inside me without judgment and censure. The committee of critics in my brain began to fade away. Slowly not fitting in became tolerable, sometimes even "nice." As AA members say, "I began to feel comfortable in my own skin." Not believing wasn't so bad. I experienced a growing interior freedom, and the fear that had ruled my life began to disappear.

I continue to try to listen and observe my inner life without jumping to conclusions or resorting to old answers. My old sense of God has not returned. Instead I seem to have settled into a sense of awe at the mystery of it all. I read scientific material (dumbed down of course). I am exploring non-objective art. A therapist would probably have a field day with that turning point. I'm now more moved by color and less by drawing. I still read books on spirituality from time to time, but I'm no longer so delusional as to believe I'll ever understand what we call God, a Higher Power, etc.

Woody Allen once said, as best I remember, "How could I figure out God when I can't even find my way around Chinatown?" With chopsticks at hand, I remain Bob Semans, class of '60.

Bob Semans (California Province 1960–73) is an artist who is no longer waiting for his old sense of God to return. A selection of his paintings is on display online at http://americangallery.wordpress.com/2012/02/29/robert-semans.

Fall Experiment: Moving Towards Vows

Lucas Sharma, nSJ

The Jesuit novitiate is a two-year period for men to enter Jesuit life, live in community, grow in relationship with Jesus, and ultimately discern whether this initial call is indeed a lifelong call. During these two years, we question who we are—looking into the depths of our souls to understand ourselves and our relationship to God. It is what beloved Jesuit Miguel Kennedy calls deep-sea diving—swimming into territory we are not even cognizant exists in the core of who we are. It is the beginning of a lifetime of profound growth and discovery. In the first year, this process began through many experiences in Los Angeles—working with young people in juvenile hall, in hospital chaplain ministry, with children at our parish school, Dolores Mission School, living in Boyle Heights with the Jesuits there, and of course, experiencing the month-long silent Spiritual Exercises Retreat. Through all these experiences, there has been a continual pattern of grace directing me out from myself and into a more intimate relationship with God and those around me.

During the second year of novitiate, we are sent out into new communities in the West Coast Province to continue discerning whether this life is truly for us. In October, I was sent to Seattle to live at L'Arche Seattle, a home for men and women with developmental disabilities. However, after receiving news of a surprise diagnosis of Stage 5 Kidney Failure, I moved into the Seattle University Jesuit community. The doctors are certain that my kidneys are operating at approximately ten percent capacity and, ultimately, will continue to deteriorate. Consequently, I've begun daily dialysis treatments and am now in the process of getting on the kidney transplant list.

In this difficult transition, I've found grace most evident in the support I've found from my family and friends.

Fall Experiment: Moving Towards Vows

This love and support is a profound grace that grants me deep consolation during this new journey. I think, though, the larger transition here is how I've continued to watch my identity as a Jesuit evolve and ripen.

In the novitiate, during our first couple of days, we were told that the Society would provide us all that we needed, not all that we wanted. I've found this to be more deeply true than I could have ever imagined—my Jesuit community here at Seattle University has gone out of its way to care for my physical, emotional, and spiritual needs. I've been touched by the deep level of love and compassion shown by all of my superiors in the process. And, perhaps most moving for me, I've experienced a radical love from my novice classmates who, through their support, continue to point me towards Jesus.

With the challenges associated with this new lifelong disease, it's tempting to become discouraged, bitter, and saddened by the treatment, the news, and the current trajectory I'm on. I would be dishonest if I pretended I hadn't felt any of those emotions over the last six weeks. Yet, what continues to fill me with joy is this continued pattern of grace—the reorienting of my heart towards Jesus and others. I am left with profound gratitude for the novitiate, for the Society, and for the love of Jesus and of my many friends, family, and brother Jesuits. In these moments of gratitude, I see this experience as less a transition into kidney failure and more an invitation to love others as a vowed Jesuit continuing through formation.

Since the writing of this piece, Lucas Sharma, nSJ, (California Province 2012) thankfully has received a kidney transplant from a close Gonzaga University friend. He is scheduled to make first vows in August 2014 and head to philosophy studies at Fordham University.

Steppingstones of Life
Images To Start My Intensive Journal

Carl J. Slawski

First grade, first day, fear—rows of strange faces, name change Jim to Carl,
Even Benigna, a kind nun in black and white costume.
Second grade, broken leg, hospital weeks, wheelchair six months.
Public school, fifth grade, little empathy, prejudice by some teachers.
Junior high, follow crowds, large classes, fit in;
Avoided perversions by boys in bus #3 and scout camp.
Move to Venice, California, from Ohio,
learned four years with Irish Catholic teachers,
catechism spirituality, led to some solace from bad marriage of parents.
First summer job as film delivery boy.
Loyola U. frosh: strained over physics, chemistry, analytic geometry,
and calculus along with English composition, debate and tennis.
Followed long black line for first four years in salubrious Los Gatos,
Easy meditation, silence, grape picking, making election, Lumina notes.
Separation trauma of third year juniorate induced by prejudiced new rector,
socially and organizationally ignorant.
Emotional scars and PTSD symptoms recurred for years.
Learned to skirt anxiety occasions via self-help addiction.

Vocation tersely dictated "lost" by Provincial after cold Spokane winter;
Word came from Rome on April Fool's Day 1963.
Began sociology in summer of '63 at Berkeley, UCLA statistics,
Then USC-AB (1964). Struggled beyond status-seeking profs
For MA at UCSB (1966); PhD at mostly welcoming U. of Illinois (1969).
Dug into GST which ballooned into collected papers around GSST, "General Social System Theories."
First academic job at Wayne State in third-world Detroit.
Spread theoretical wings at U. of Toronto summer school (1969),
The time during which we humans landed on the moon.
Wrote "Elements of Loving," and later "Love, Power and Conflict,"
Which led to eventual two volumes on theory and practice
For marriage and relationship counseling.
Short non-welcome mat at CSC-Long Beach.
Student evaluation of teacher data prompted grievances and
"Open Systems for Learning"
collected papers.
Took Munich year to write, and then use up Eurail Pass, Arctic to Marathon;
Polishing there my "Evaluating Theories Comparatively,"
focusing on GSST, charts and chaos (non-linear dynamics) theories.
Taught 24 courses altogether (social psych. from my handbook,
theory, small groups, conflict, science, and religion in biography) but

Back at LB ranch endured four "saving," then three "parting" grievances.

Prostate cancer diagnosis led to 38 proton treatments, paid out of pocket $35,000.

Bucked HMO (KP, Kaiser-Permanente, and Blue Shield) to a dead-end state Supreme Court,

Watched father wither from T-cell cancer, mother from heart failure from smoking,
along with her naivete toward a sweetheart swindler.

Solidified "BUREAU-cratitis" theory and practice ideas.

Married at 60 to long-lost friend and good companion, a teacher of high school English and film.

Fractured skull from bike fall before Christmas (2007)
in Thousand Oaks on Windtree,

Giving brief dizzy spells for a year and a half.

Solidified need for sorting papers, preparing for the end of life,

Clarifying images of earth, galaxies, creation, legacy, and afterlife.

Ending with implicit (sociology of knowledge based) reinterpretation:
the sign of the cross in God's three functions:

"In the name of the Creator, the Redeemer, and the Spirit of Life."

Carl Slawski (California Province 1957–63) taught General Social System Theories for many years. Companions' exchanges help keep up his interest in church politics, spirituality, and theological issues. His future tasks will include elaboration in the twenty-five or more sections of the Intensive Journal through imagery and inventive dialogues with persons, works, society, events, the body, and inner wisdom figures.

Late Night Thoughts on Leaving JRS

Gary N. Smith, SJ

"One never reaches home," she said. "But where paths that have affinity for each other intersect, the whole world looks like home for a time."
From *Demian*, by Herman Hesse

On Loss and Blessing

We stood there, the three of us, on a dusty road in the Kakuma Refugee Camp in northern Kenya. I was with two Sudanese refugees, tall young men, Peter and Zachariah, leaders in one of the Catholic Chapels in which I serve. I told them that I would be leaving Kakuma and Africa soon. Probably for good. As best as I could, I told them why. They absorbed the news thoughtfully. In their lives the notion of loss and blessing often come together. They told me that they knew I loved their people and that the people loved me, but they understood that this movement in my heart was strong and that my reasons for leaving were sound. In their eyes, all of this was of God. They felt my presence with them has been a blessing from God even as my absence will be a loss. It was one of those unforgettable conversations one has in life; an inner icon to which the heart must return periodically and contemplate.

Arrupe's Vision

In the late nineties, while living in Portland, Oregon, I decided to move from ministry in the streets of the USA to the streets of the world. I pondered once again the vision of Fr. Pedro Arrupe, Superior General of the Society of Jesus, the Jesuits. In the eighties he decided to take the Jesuits in a new direction. It was this: that the Jesuits, in a vast, universal, full-speed-ahead move toward the poor, should embrace the cause of the refugees of the world. He wanted the Society of Jesus to commit itself to accompanying them in whatever way possible. The scope and implications of this proposal were breathtaking. But would Jesuits do it? Would it be possible to summon from the heart of the Society of Jesus the skills and faith which could be systematically hurled into the breaches of human suffering synonymous with the flight and plight of refugees?

Arrupe never doubted it could be done. A way of proceeding was created: the organization that was born would eventually be called The Jesuit Refugee Service (JRS). And then there is this: Arrupe knew that the Society of Jesus is healthiest, at its best, when it is with the poor, with the marginalized. JRS would take the Jesuits and its lay collaborators into the thick of poverty in the battle for the dignity and rights of refugees. With the poor the Society of Jesus would discover once again what it longs to be, would uncover again its deepest desire: taking the risky march into the unknown to be with those who have—at least by the world's standards—no power, no money and no beauty. In that tentative world the Society of Jesus would follow, imitate and bet its life on the poor Christ.

Beginnings

By 1999, nearly twenty years after the Jesuits established JRS, the world-wide refugee numbers had not diminished, but increased. By millions. I approached JRS. Can you use me? We can; we need someone in East Africa. I talked it over with my Provincial. Go with my blessing he said. I was in.

I started in the Rhino Camp Refugee Settlements, Northern Uganda, on the West Nile with Sudanese refugees, later moving to Adjumani and Palorinya Refugee Settlements, Uganda, again with Sudanese. From there I went to Makhado, South Africa, on the border of Zimbabwe, attending and serving Zimbabwean refugees. As this is written, my current assignment is with the JRS project at the Kakuma Refugee Camp, Kenya, a Camp containing refugees from several East Africa countries: Sudan, Ethiopia, Somalia, Eritrea, Congo, Rwanda, Burundi, and Uganda among others. More than 90,000 people.

Twelve years have passed. Growth and life. Wear and tear. Success. Failure. I've entered unimaginable worlds of learning and love. In it all I have discovered more deeply the heart of God working in me, in those around me and in the JRS mission. Seems like a wonderful discovery. It is.

Moments

In Uganda, in South Africa, in Kenya, in Sudan I've experienced things hard to believe.

I've seen destroyed huts and lifeless bodies in Pakelle, murdered by the Lord's Resistance Army (LRA).

Held the reassuring hand of 11-year-old Sudanese refugee, Regina, escorting me through the labyrinthine earthen streets of Kakuma.

Wept at the humility of Zimbabwean refugees, offering their morning prayers of thanksgiving. Their sole possession: the clothes on their back.

I've watched Chameleons creeping among the burnt out buildings of Barituku.

Shared with Somali students in Kakuma, of their Islamic faith and their flight from Somalia.

Felt the fear of Nimule Southern Sudanese as we heard the approaching drone of Antonov bombers.

I have known Jesuits—simply the best—who backed me, laughed with me, cried with me, believed in me.

Late Night Thoughts on Leaving JRS

Seen thousands of armed Sudan People's Liberation Army (SPLA) troops moving outside of Moyo. Witnessed babies born on the beds of pick-up trucks and beneath the gigantic leaves of Teak trees.

I've taught refugee catechists and rejoiced as they unlocked the mysteries of Faith to their people. Grasped the fingerless hands of begging lepers in the market place of Arua.

Seen terror on the remembering faces of Rwandan, Burundian, and Congolese women.

I've witnessed the spectacular dance of celebration by the ululating Dinka women of Miriye.

Gazed at the elephantine Baobab trees, guarding the road from Makhado to Zimbabwe.

Remember the laughter of Atibuni and Asega in Rhino Camp, of Peninah in Kakuma, of Frido and Atimango in Adjumani, and of Thandi and the entire irrepressible JRS team in Makhado.

From dusk to dawn I've listened to inconsolable refugee mothers of Yoro mourning their lost children.

Experienced the first malaria attack, an unyielding tsunami breaching my shores.

Endured the sting and heartache of confrontations and unresolved disagreements with JRS staff.

I've been consoled by the sunsets of Kakuma, the early morning mist rising off the Nile and the Southern Cross glittering in the Johannesburg nights.

I have smelled the roses in a Nairobi morning and the earth after a South African rain.

Turned my face into the warm winds of Kampala blowing off of Lake Victoria.

Listened to the night breezes moving through the Neem trees of Rhino Camp.

Deep in the bush, I've taken malarial babies—hours away from death—in my arms and kissed them.

Held the faith-filled hands of blind and crippled Yayo in Magburu as she said goodbye to me.

Comforted Makhado refugee, Mandinyenya, weeping over news of his mother's death in Zimbabwe.

I've celebrated Mass beneath trees in countless villages, in chapels and in small rooms; occasions filled with the transparent faith and passion that inhabits and powers the African Church.

From Johannesburg to Juba I've been captured by refugee children, whose happy greetings surely could be heard in the Kingdom of the Deaf and whose smiles could light up my darkness night.

Each day I have been nourished by the faith and wisdom and hope and love of refugees.

Each African morning—thousands of them—I awoke knowing that God waited for me. And desired me.

Many moments expressed; many beyond words: all Way Stations on the road toward what is true and good, and toward the One who authors the miracle of my life and whose mystery is beyond expression.

Struggles

I've learned that JRS is not made up of a bunch of saints. It is an organization that can bleed; it has its flaws and imperfections; its leaders struggle with the implementation of its principles and goals. It must gently listen to the impelling Spirit of God, and embrace change, and not fear mid-course adjustments. Its staffs must regularly evaluate why they do what they do; JRS must help them nourish their spirituality; calling them more deeply to understanding the foundations of their accompaniment and service of and advocacy for refugees. Instinctively, JRS must always—

Late Night Thoughts on Leaving JRS

always—be in the hunt for its roots and for Arrupe's epiphany and driven by his sense of indignation. Something like this: There are people who are suffering and hurting and they are alone. This is wrong. They have the dignity of God's children. We must be in solidarity with them. We must act.

Finding Home

There is a rising wrenching sadness in me, though it is clear, for personal reasons, that it is time to go. Leaving refugees is a difficult chalice to drink. But countering the sadness there is—as Peter and Zachariah would say—a blessing from God. I am like the person who ascends the mountain and looks back, with love, down at the country that has been traversed. From the top of the mountain the world looks so different; a person's perspective changes in twelve years of daily, personal encounters with goodness. There is loss, but it walks hand in hand with blessing.

One never reaches home, but for a time, while living among the refugees, my heart always found a home.

Jesuit Refugee Service,
Kakuma Refugee Camp, Northern Kenya

Gary Smith, SJ, joined the Oregon Province in 1959 and has spent his life doing justice in the world described in this story.

"The Child in My Womb Leapt for Joy."

J. Michael Sparough, SJ

Like a bolt of lightning briefly illumines a night sky, so did this moment light the way to the path I have been walking ever since. In the spring of 1969, we Jesuits of the Chicago Province under Fr. Bob Harvanek were beginning a detailed re-examination of our ministries. What should be kept and what should we let go of as we respond to "the signs of the times" in the wake of the *aggiornamento* of Vatican II?

Delegates were elected to represent the men from across the stretches of the Province, and we gathered for several days at a retreat house outside Chicago. I was a second year novice at the time, and we were employed as the underlings to do all the messy little detail work to keep the conference running smoothly.

Just shy of my nineteenth birthday, and a bit awed to be in the presence of the "big guns" of our Jesuit Province, I was excited to be a part of the action. Only there was no action, just plenty of drama. The question the delegates got mired in was whether to close St. Ignatius College Prep—that noble institution founded by Father Arnold Damen, who first brought the Jesuits to the Chicago area. SICP was losing money; it was located in a dicey neighborhood with some of the most violent housing projects located across the street. Enrollment was slipping, and some of the Jesuits had been threatened by neighborhood thugs. With fewer vocations rolling in, the question was put on the table: Shall we close the high school and move into other more progressive ministries?

"The Child in My Womb Leapt for Joy."

The debate was heated, and the two opposing camps battered each other with the full force of Jesuitical rhetoric. It was not our finest hour. A young bearded scholastic raised his hand to speak. Once recognized by the chair, he leapt onto the table. An explosion of sound and movement enveloped the room.

    SURR-GERR-GERR   URR-GERR-GERR
    WOOOOSSH!
    ZZZZZA-TELL-A-TEE PIT- IT
    KA-ROAR-IK   KA-ROAR-IK
    JEL-KA-MA-RU- NEE - KA-PLUT
    FLIT.
    WOOOOOOOSH!

Eyeballs rolled, but no one moved. Air rushing into the room from the heating ducts was the only sound heard. The hairs on my neck stood at attention.

Ken Feit was well known to this group. He called himself a "fool" in the medieval and biblical sense of the term. Some just thought him a fool—period. But here he was performing one of his "sound poems," a collection of onomatopoetic nonsense that told a story. Ken proffered an explanation in rhythmic speech and gesture:

A sputtering motorboat is running out of gas. Naysayer frogs croak in the thrushes, while hissing water spiders weave webs of despair. Facing empty nets, disgruntled fishermen throw their decomposing bait into the water. Fear reigns as startled critics leap for cover. Only mud rises from the inky bottom.

A parable in sound and motion in the midst of our fury. The chair of the conference wisely did the only thing he could do. He called for a recess to "consider these matters."

J. Michael Sparough, SJ

The pause was more than pregnant. I felt like Elizabeth carrying John the Baptist. The child in my womb leapt for joy, and I didn't even know I was pregnant. There was a part of me that awakened that day, a part of me I didn't know was asleep. I had always been good in science and math. I entered the Jesuits wanting to be a brain surgeon. I had no real interest in drama. I was passionate about sports, not poetry.

This "fool" entered quite unexpectedly into my life, speaking another language, a language some part of me immediately understood, although I had never studied it. It was like connecting with your long lost sibling you never knew you had. Ken became my mentor, me the "aspiring fool." I started taking classes in theatre and dance and writing poetry. I gave up my dream of a life in medicine.

Ken's sound poem cleared the air not just in that assembly room but also in my soul. After the recess, with calmer spirits, the Jesuit delegates reconsidered, and it was decided that the high school would continue to be a priority ministry for our Province. It flourishes today. As for me, forty-five years later, I continue my ministry of listening to and telling stories, crafting poems, and practicing medicine as doctor to the soul. I'm forever an apprentice to that FOOL we hung on a tree so long ago.

Mike Sparough, SJ, (Chicago-Detroit Province 1968) is a storyteller, writer, retreat master, and spiritual director at the Bellarmine Retreat House. He is the founder of Charis Ministries, a Jesuit outreach to young adults. He is also the founder and former artistic director of the Fountain Square Fools, a religious performing arts ensemble. His latest book What's Your Decision? *is published by Loyola Press.*

"B" Students Also Admitted

James R. Stickney

When new acquaintances discover that I spent 17 years in the Society of Jesus, they often exclaim how brilliant Jesuits are—"the best educated of the Catholic orders." Then a pause ensues, during which they wait for some sage erudition or repartee to justify their compliment. When I reply that the Society also admitted novices who were "B" students along with the academic superstars, they either nod at my assumed false humility, or they take my words at face value and move along, as much as to say, "How 'bout them 'Niners?"

For new acquaintances who stay around, though, I tell them that if one is going to serve as a Roman Catholic priest, he should be a Jesuit!

When I entered in 1963, Vatican II was well under way. After the rigors of novitiate, I had the sense that, along with my comrades, we were going to change the church from within. By the time I studied theology at Berkeley, those classmates who remained seemed eager (as I imagined) for women priests, married priests, and much more voice given to lay leaders in the church. We were all waiting for "that conservative", Paul VI, to be taken into heaven so that "the new Pope" would usher in the radical changes of Vatican II.

But when Pope John Paul II was elected, my disillusionment deepened, and I saw a lonely future. Celibacy (always a struggle) was greatly tested. I had seen older Jesuits who took refuge in drink, and my own toking a joint of weekend marijuana was not much different.

Episcopal friends in Berkeley had introduced me to their church, and I now felt called to become an

Episcopal priest. I met with the Provincial to discuss it, and after our meeting in Los Gatos, I climbed to the roof of the old novitiate building and wept. But after Easter of 1980, I began the transition.

So I gave up the security of knowing I'd always be employed. I became a word-processor for a Silicon Valley law firm, and I became a married man. My smoking grass dropped to zero and stayed zero. But it took six long years to find a full-time position as an Episcopal priest.

There were two periods when my Jesuit background proved invaluable in the Episcopal Church. First, in a parish when a couple of gossipmongers conspired to have me squeezed out as Rector, I endured direct rudeness and calumny for more than a year before the crisis passed. I tapped into some residual stamina from the Examen:

> {Jesuits} desire to clothe themselves with the same uniform and clothing of Christ our Lord . . . to such an extent that . . . they would wish to suffer injuries, false accusations, and affronts, and to be held and esteemed as fools (but without their giving any occasion for this), because of their desire to resemble and imitate in some manner our Lord and Savior Jesus Christ.

So this ex-Jesuit took the high road—I endured it all without descending to the level of my adversaries. (At least they couldn't crucify me!) I found the wisdom of that Psalm refrain, which sings "my enemies have dug a pit for me, and have fallen into it themselves." Most parishioners declined to join a church fight, my adversaries lost credibility, and the parish was healthier after the conflict ended.

There was a second, more crucial way, in which my Jesuit background has served the Episcopal Church. When I turned 60, I felt called to serve as an interim in Episcopal churches that had gone through crisis. In the Central Valley of California (the "red state" inside our "blue state") the previous "charismatic" bishop had taken many parishes into schism over issues like our church's ordination of women, gay clergy, and the blessings of same-sex marriages.

Some parishes that remained Episcopal needed an interim pastor who could deal with external conflict without making things worse internally. I felt the Two Standards from the Spiritual Exercises snap into place. "O God, please find me worthy to be sent into those places where the spiritual struggle is the toughest." The Episcopal Church was under siege, this community that gave me a future when I left the Roman Catholic Church. How could I not respond? After all, the Episcopal Church resembles the church of my birth, had it been radically reformed—with laity having a strong voice to decide about its clergy (male or female) and the incorporation of gay and lesbian Christians.

So this "B" student has brought Jesuit training to help the Episcopal Church fulfill its unique ministry. It's about much more than getting married, or enjoying classical music on Sunday. I've served Christ Jesus with a fuller heart in this branch of Christ's church. Thanks be to God!

Jim Stickney joined the Jesuits of the California Province in 1963, was ordained a priest in 1975, and joined the Episcopal Church in 1980. In 1986 he was called to serve at St. Alban's Church in Albany, California (just north of Berkeley) where he was the Rector for two decades. For the last seven years he served as an interim priest, principally in California's Central Valley. Jim retired in December of 2013, and lives in El Cerrito, California with his wife Joni. Jim's new avocation is stained glass, with which he plans to start a new business.

The Problem

John F. Suggs

When I was a student at St. Catherine's Elementary School in Riverside, California in the 1960s and early 1970s, my all-time favorite game to play at recess was a seemingly benign game of über-tag.

The game was rather simple to play, requiring only a football and the active participation of a group of boys from my class. We would play it on the dirt field next to the school's blacktop playground. The game would begin with someone throwing the football high up in the air and whoever caught the ball became "it." All the boys would then give chase to the boy with the ball until he was finally caught and tackled. Once he was down, as a group, we would then give him an unrestrained beating, punching and kicking him with the goal of forcing him to drop the football. After we all finished getting in our licks, and if the boy had shown that he was "tough enough" to take our beatings and not drop the football, he was then helped back up to his feet and allowed to throw the ball in the air for someone else to catch, and the process would be repeated again and again until we heard the bell announcing the end of recess.

Whenever we played, I loved being "it" and delighted in my ability to show both myself and my buddies that I could take their beatings without weakly "giving up the football" to stop the pummeling.

I never really gave much thought about that child's game until years later when I was in the second year of my Jesuit novitiate. As part of my training, I had been sent to work as a hospital chaplain at Los Angeles County USC General

The Problem

Hospital. County General, both then and now, serves as the primary source of medical care for people in Los Angeles who are uninsured, homeless, undocumented, or just plain poor. My Jesuit superiors had sent me there to train, instead of to a more upscale Catholic hospital, because of our shared commitment to the ideal of a "preferential option for the poor" and living a "faith that does justice."

I frequently found myself working with patients who were not much older than I (twenty-four years old)—or even younger—who were sick and dying from illnesses related to a rather new disease called AIDS. A lot of these young men arrived at the hospital virtually destitute. Of those who were destitute, many had become estranged from their parents and other family members after coming out as gay men.

One night after work, as I made my regular evening prayers in the empty chapel at Dolores Mission in East L.A. where I was living, I reflected on what one of my AIDS patients had shared with me that afternoon. He was a young man who told me his all-too-familiar story about his estrangement from his family. He shared that his father had once said to him in a fit of anger that he would rather his son were dead than gay. He then let out a rueful laugh and bitterly noted that his father was soon going to get his wish.

As I prayed for both him and his father, I suddenly found myself remembering that long ago childhood game. And as I did, I realized, with a start, what it was that we were really doing out on that dirt field at St. Catherine's. The truth had been hiding in plain sight all along. For you see, the name of our game was "Smear the Queer." What we were doing was "playing at" assaulting gay men, gay bashing. The boy with the football was our "designated queer," and everyone else was expected to tackle him, hit him, and kick him until he gave up the football and "stopped being queer."

I remember sitting in that empty chapel, stunned, as the realization of the meaning behind our "innocent" kids game first became clear to me. This was rapidly followed by a second and even more disturbing insight. For I vividly recalled how, as we boys would all rush out of our classrooms at the start of recess eagerly calling out the name of the game at the top of our lungs to enlist others to play it with us, no adult, not a single Sister, no playground supervisor, no parent, no coach, nor the parish priest, ever spoke up and told us that our "game" was hurtful or "unchristian" and that we must stop. No one. Not once.

That deafening silence, from virtually all the responsible adults in our young lives, will always stand as Exhibit A in my stipulation that I was raised in a culture suffused with homophobia. This homophobic culture was such that fathers would actually disown their own sons and wish them dead rather than alive and gay.

The destructive influence of this cultural homophobia fueled my five-year-long struggle to make my decision to apply and enter the Jesuits. Its corrosiveness would further threaten to upend my entrance and my initial training as a Jesuit novice. Only as I gradually progressed through the difficult, yet extraordinary training as a Jesuit was I able to come to terms with and exorcize my own deeply rooted cultural homophobia.

Consider: One afternoon during my spring semester as a senior at Loyola Marymount University, I was hanging out with my Jesuit mentor and friend Tom Higgins, SJ. We were sitting in his campus apartment watching a game together on his beat up second-hand TV. I was nervous (read: scared to death!) and he was distracted by the game, and utterly oblivious to the importance of what I was about to share with him. Finally, when I could stand the suspense no longer, I anxiously blurted out, "Alright God Dammit, I will do it! " He looked up quizzically from the TV, turned to me and asked, "Do what?" Exasperated by his question, I replied even more forcefully: "Join the Jesuits, dammit!"

His reaction? He paused for a second; my heart skipping a beat while he took in what I had just said and then slowly started to chuckle. The chuckle was quickly followed with him bursting out laughing. Eventually, he was laughing so hard and uncontrollably that he literally fell off his chair. Granted, this was not exactly the response I had been anticipating, but it was pure Higs—funny, authentic, and original. And before I knew it I, too, was laughing.

Higs and I would talk of many things that afternoon but we never once talked about what was behind the obvious distress in my decision. We didn't have to; the reason for my discomfort was explicitly understood between us. It was because of a "problem" that both of us fully recognized and accepted as a "problem." What I was grudgingly telling Higs was that, in spite of the "problem," I would, nevertheless, join the Jesuits. Hence my unconcealed exasperation and our mutual gallows humor.

Because of the "problem," the mere idea of actually disclosing to my family and friends that I was interested in becoming a Catholic priest filled me with an overwhelming sense of anxiety and dread. For a time I managed to half convince myself that my extreme, visceral, negative reaction was because my faith and spirituality was an intensely private matter that I did not easily "wear on my sleeve." But that wasn't the truth. It would only be later, after I had finally given up the fight and actually done "that which I feared the most here and now," i.e., entering the California Province novitiate, that I first began to catch glimpses of just how much my fear and dread of becoming a priest was grounded in something considerably more primitive, unappealing and threatening; for the "problem" was the realization that, at that point in time, wanting to be a young, celibate Jesuit priest was tantamount to declaring oneself a gay man.

Due to my own personal homophobia at that time, this realization posed several "problems" for me, the first being that even though I was not gay, I still, most adamantly, did not want to be thought of as gay. Nor did I have any interest "whatsoever!" in spending the rest of my life living in community with a bunch of gay men. And yet, even though I was quite clear on these two points, try as I might, I simply couldn't escape this enduring desire to become a Jesuit Priest. I was stuck, and both Higs and I knew it.

With very few role models to help guide me, and with great trepidation, I entered the novitiate. Not surprisingly under the circumstances, my "on-boarding" as a novice quickly proved difficult. My typical feeling state was one of confusion and uncertainty. It seemed as if, with every passing day, I would inadvertently say or do something else wrong. I would only realize later that it was my cultural homophobia that was at the heart of my sense of fear and ill ease as I transitioned into being a novice.

At the end of each of those long first days I would return to my small room and lock myself in for the night. In the morning I would sit silently for the longest time just staring at my closed locked door. It would often take all the courage I had just to stand up, open the door and walk back out for yet another day of this painful adjustment. Not surprisingly, in my uneasiness during the course of those initial days

The Problem

and first weeks, I quickly racked up not one but two nicknames.

My first novitiate nickname, "Citizen Suggs", was bestowed upon me rather quickly by my Novice Master, Wilkie Au, SJ, after he discovered that during my first few days I had responded to my growing discomfort by instinctively channeling my energy into an arena where I was certain of quickly regaining a sense of mastery and control. Not only was it something that I was naturally quite good at, but as an added bonus, it would also offer me the fun of "tweaking the noses" of the novitiate administration: I started an organizing campaign to unionize the novitiate's three ground maintenance workers.

Wilkie promptly called me in to his office and, politely but firmly, ordered me to cease my organizing efforts and instead to refocus on my own novice program. After first securing an agreement from him that he would fully address any worker grievances that might yet surface as a result of the organizing efforts (again, "mastery and control"), I agreed to stand down. Afterwards, whenever we would pass each other in the halls, I would grin and give him a raised fist salute while stating a pro-union slogan or simply "To the Revolution!" In response, he would give a good-natured laugh for all to hear and call me "Citizen Suggs."

Later, Wilkie confided in me that he had intentionally given me that nickname because he was genuinely worried that I might end up alienating people in the novitiate as I struggled with making the transition. He said that he had wanted to at least give me a fighting chance to make it at the novitiate in those early days by throwing me a lifeline and modeling for the rest of the novitiate that they should react to my intensity with humor. He was right. The humor worked. (Thank you, Wilk!)

My transition continued to be rocky. Frankly, I wasn't making a very good first impression. One brief but telling example: At either my second or third dinner in the novitiate I stupidly and rather inelegantly proceeded to tell everyone at my table the true story of the farewell advice I had been given from one of my brothers-in-law. As the two of us had said our goodbyes, I told them, he pulled me aside, looked me straight in the eye and half jokingly, half seriously, warned me about how to survive the novitiate: "Always carry a knife, always keep your back to the wall and, what ever you do, John, don't ever bend over in the showers." I let out a huge laugh as I finished the story, which basically equated the novitiate with a maximum security prison where rape is routine. As I laughed, I noticed that my funny "true story" only elicited a few strained, polite smiles in return. In the months ahead, I would be embarrassed to learn that virtually every man sitting at the table that night was gay.

Which brings me to my second nickname and how I acquired it. Another day, early on, I imprudently expressed my opinion to a couple of the guys (which, of course, promptly got re-told throughout the novitiate) that I thought that only "Jesus Freaks" hugged each other at Mass during the Sign of Peace. (I wanted to say "Gays" instead of "Jesus Freaks" but I instinctively sensed that that would be crossing a line that I wasn't ready—or willing—to cross.) In those early community Masses I always reflexively stuck my hand out to shake and thus avoided ever being on the receiving end of someone else's hug. But after that wisecrack got around, my classmates decided that they had had just about enough of my offensive pronouncements, and that it was time to teach me an important lesson. So, at the Sign of Peace at the next day's Mass, my classmates surprised me by refusing my outstretched hand and, instead, gave me great big bear hugs. And as they each hugged me, they laughingly whispered in my ear "Peace, Cuddles!"

If I could point to a single moment that was the beginning of the dismantling of my cultural homophobia, it was right then, standing around our community altar in the middle of Mass, being hugged by my predominantly gay classmates while they teasingly christened me "Cuddles" in response to my aversion to being hugged.

The bulk of our second year as novices was spent living and working in different active Jesuit communities in order to gain valuable first-hand knowledge and experience. I was sent to work with lepers and tortured (literally) prisoners in Mexico, with the sick and dying at County General in East L.A., as well as with bored freshmen at a Jesuit prep school in California.

In all of these postings I typically got along well with the other Jesuits but there was one where it quickly became rather obvious that I was being deliberately excluded by a group of influential Jesuits within the community. And I didn't like it. At first, I assumed my exclusion was because I was a novice. But that explanation ceased to hold up when another novice came through and this group immediately and warmly embraced him. At that point the truth of what was behind my exclusion finally dawned on me. Not only was the other novice a gay man, but so were all those in this group. Wow! An exclusive community clique was snubbing me because I wasn't gay!

At first I was indignant. But then, as I took the matter to prayer and spiritual direction, I began to discern the important life lesson I was being taught. For in this situation, I was experiencing, for the very first time in my life, the sensation of being "The Other." I, a person who had spent every day of his life as one of the undeserving recipients of the privileges enjoyed by the very select group of highly educated, heterosexual, affluent, white male, US Citizens, was suddenly "The Other." What an amazing gift. I had quite unexpectedly (miraculously?) stumbled upon one of the very few and rare opportunities I would ever have to know, first hand, what it feels like to be excluded for something that I am and cannot change. This incredible learning opportunity was what neither Higs nor I could have ever imagined on that day not so long ago, when we fell on his floor laughing at my "predicament."

I resolved then and there to fully embrace and own "deep down in my gut" virtually every feeling and sensation associated with this utterly new and unique experience. And I swore that I would never forget this moment.

Epilogue

Several years after I had successfully finished the novitiate, two events in rapid succession showed me that the dismantling of my cultural homophobia was complete.

I was in philosophy studies at Gonzaga in the Oregon Province when I first learned the terrible news that my Novice classmate Michael Heffernan, SJ, had been sent to the Jesuit infirmary at USF and was dying of AIDS. I skipped my classes and simply cried for days. Before Mike died I visited him in the infirmary and was able to tell him, face to face, that he was the first openly gay man that I had ever known and loved (a member of my own family wouldn't come out of the closet for several more years). I shared with him how important he was to me, how much I loved him and how I treasured his friendship. We prayed together, hugged and warmly held each other, blessed each other, then parted for the last time.

Later that same year, a surprise announcement was shared with every Jesuit living within the borders of the Oregon Province. Each and every Jesuit who was assigned to an Oregonian community was ordered to report to their community that very afternoon at a specific time to hear an important message from the provincial. Everyone was wondering what it could possibly be about, but one thing was certain: it would not be good news. And, of course, it wasn't. The announcement—shared at the exact same time to every Jesuit throughout the Province—was that Peter Davis, SJ, a much beloved and well known and respected parish priest, would be giving a live press conference in the very next hour to reveal that he had recently been diagnosed with HIV-AIDS, and that he was gay. Peter would be the very first parish priest in the United States to publicly make such an announcement and, as such, it was covered as a National News Story.

What has stayed with me all these years is what happened next. The provincial's letter closed by stating that he, the provincial, would be joining Peter at his press conference, and he intended to publicly reaffirm what he was telling each of us, his fellow Jesuits, at this moment, that we Jesuits are Peter's brothers, and that the entire Oregon Province stands proudly and unequivocally beside him today and all the days ahead. In essence, he was telling each of us and the larger public, that if anyone should so much as dare to judge or attack Peter because he was coming out as a gay man that they would first have to answer to all of us who, to a man, stood in solidarity with him.

It was my proudest moment as a Jesuit.

John F. Suggs (California Province 1984–89) works as an Investigative Genealogist helping adopted adults who are looking for their birth families. He lives with his wife Sharon and their eleven-year-old twins Rachel and Joshua in Westport, Connecticut.

Segue

William M. Sullivan

Replaying the cinemascope of my transitions, they seem more like segues dissolving into each other, perhaps directed by Orson Welles or Federico Fellini. I'm having fun with that in the middle of my eight-day retreat under the direction of a Jesuit Zen Master at the Bodhi Zendo in the hills of South India. Forty-one years ago, I did my first Zen retreat with the first Jesuit Zen Master, Enomiya Lasalle, who survived the Hiroshima bomb and mentored my current director, AMA Swamy, who yesterday told the America college student group I am with, "Be Christ, be Buddha." Three years ago, he told me: "Say yes to life, that's all!" Today, I reminded him of that and he laughed and added: "and death and everything else to learn to love."

I left the Jesuits in 1973 after completing the full "formation", and after the Rector had declared me a "heretic," and the Provincial added: "We can't trust you," because I had exposed his collusion with the Bishop of Fresno and agribusiness against César Chávez and the Farmworkers' Union. They both would have added another word if they had known about my girlfriend. Those were the great Berkeley years when Ronnie Reagan sent in helicopters to spray us with tear gas, and deputies swung clubs, but the Vietnam War did stop. I moved to LA for a job with Marymount Palos Verdes College. They hired me because I could teach in two departments: film and theology & philosophy. Still, I didn't have a clue when a student in one of my courses asked me about Sri Aurobindo. After educating myself fast, my astonishment grew at discovering a brilliant mystic with a vision for the earth who was also a political revolutionary (seeded the freedom of India), a philosopher who created an integral yoga for a transformation of the human species, and a poet. I had no choice but to return to a country I had already visited once condemning it as a hopeless mess, vowing never to return.

Sri Aurobindo died in 1950 and his spiritual collaborator, Mirra Alfassa who became known as the Mother, founded Auroville in 1968 as "the city of dawn, the city the earth needs." I arrived in 1974; it was a perfect place for me. In recent years, I have even gone back to the old job I had as a scholastic at Xavier in Manila: teaching English Lit to high school seniors. Now, I am also building the Trash Mahal as a home out of waste material (Earth-ship style) part of the Zero Waste Auroville movement. Endlessly enjoyable tasks here where the laborers are few but the harvest is great.

I think it is in Eckhart Tolle's magnificent book, *A New Earth*, where he tells the story of J. Krishnamurti finally agreeing to tell his followers the secret of his enlightenment. He disclosed: "I don't mind." Last month, a goddess-like gift from the universe cuddled up to me and whispered: "Do you mind if I take my bra off?" In my shock and awe, I could still manage to mumble: "I don't mind." I am loving her *per omnia saecula saeculorum*. Now, eternally grateful at seventy-three to be feeling thirteen, and thanking Bob Holstein (ora pro nobis), RRR, and Brother Van Etten, and you, Don, for our Compañeros connections. How could we have anticipated that the Mystical Body of Christ would manifest as the Internet, and Google become the Holy Spirit where all is forever accessible? Amen.

B William Sullivan (his Facebook name)—just B to his friends—was in the California Province from 1960 to 1973. He is now laboring on the Trash Mahal and thanking the universe for gifts bestowed.

Through the Ordinary

Patrick J. Twohy, SJ

It is through the ordinary,
through ordinary eyes and hands,
through our flesh and blood
and the flesh and blood of our children,
that a Great Power comes into the world.
Through simple lives, humble and forgotten,
the Spirit races through the world
touching everyone, touching everything
with a sovereign dignity, with a forgetfulness of self,
surrounding all with an incomprehensible Silence
that for those who hear it becomes
the sound of spirits singing.
And it does not matter whether we move
forward or backward in time,
flesh and blood are there,
and the Silence,
and this immense Song
which we, too, can sing
if only we allow it to enter
our ordinary bodies and change us
into something entirely new.

Pat Twohy, SJ, (Oregon Province 1957) is a man who has spent many decades accompanying, ministering with, and being ministered to by Native Americans in the Pacific Northwest. His poem was published in the March 2014 issue of the Oregon/California Social Ministries Newsletter.

Then There Is Family

Mary Ann & Dave Van Etten

At the ripeness of days we declared all vows.
Our one voice whispered: "I leave, now, this home,
This life, for God is there, there in the mouths
Of migrants, students, disabled children—
There the sunshine distills through the leaves—
There, in Taiwan and Kentucky, Brophy and Kankakee,
Is where I share in the Spirit. Where hope
Is not stolen."
And at the ripeness of days our spirits were stolen,
Our spirit was found. We hushed our hearts awake
And vowed
To God and each other: "A family, a new home
Is born." The Colorado grasses were mouths
Whispering joy and untepid. All of the children
(as much amazed) were wonder disguised
As family, friends. We left
Through a new door. And hope was the key.
Our marriage grew, ripe with days and keys
And, yes, butterflies and daisies, as if God
Had stolen
All hope from the heavens, to collect in a whisper,
A vow:
"A child is born, Mary Grace" from the mouth
Of some unknown river, and then "David" —
Almost unknown miracles, these children
Laughing, weeping, strong as the leaves.
Then it was sunshine. This family grew green and strong:
Strong as a play box with warm voices always left
Playing, in Playtime—strong as twenty-five years—
Strong as twenty-five copper keys
Sleeping on a Kitchen table—strong and wondrous,
Like the stolen
Breaths of napping children . . . We have softly grown
Into four Van Etten children whose vows

Then There Is Family

Are made of dreams and whose dreams themselves
Are so many hopeful mouths—
Whose dreams themselves
Are so many passionate children.
The ripeness of years have filtered sunshine
Into other children.
We have sold them homes; we have given them homes,
So many earth-faced children, god-faced children who leave
702 Cree Drive with river in their blood.
We have taken Latch-Key
Children and Latch-Key parents and stolen
Back their hope, stolen into their lives:
With world we have made our vow.
And the Van Etten home has given the Spirit
A mouth.
In retired years we open our mouths
In communion. Full of life and as children
We walk onward, morningward, we flow like leaves
Greenward, like water seaward, and the key
To all of this, the missing part, the stolen
Answer breathes within each one of us, whispering,
The pulse of a vow
That is family; leave that child
There, asleep, awake; that mouth speaks in a melodious key,
A tender strumming, a music that is our vow,
Forever: the ripeness of hope is here, unstolen.

Dave Van Etten (California Province 1958–69) and his wife Mary Ann have been wonderfully involved in their work as daycare providers (finally winding down after decades), and many projects and collaborations involving Jesuits and former Jesuits. For more than fifteen years Dave has been a director of West Coast Compañeros, Inc. (WCCI), serving as Chief Financial Officer and Reunion Coordinator extraordinare.

Personal Statement
LSAC Account # L25170166

David W. Van Etten

My mother was a nun and my father was a Jesuit when they met each other at the University of San Francisco taking summer classes in 1967. Like many other men and women filled with the idealism of that post-Vatican II era, my parents left religious life together to start a family and attempt good works in secular society. About fifteen years behind their suburban peers financially, they managed to buy a house in San Jose and start a home daycare business, where my sister and I were raised. Growing up the son of the neighborhood baby-sitters is democratizing and somehow prototypically American: you are special and yet simultaneously one amongst many, constantly welcoming newcomers, celebrating individualism while upholding the ideal of sharing. My merits as a student and my values as a future lawyer took shape in that household where everyone knew how to hold a baby bottle and change a diaper. The qualities of consistency and civic responsibility, which are the basis of my future law career, were simply part of the family business.

The life-blood of the home daycare business is consistency. My parents have cared for a rotating group of twelve children over the years, each child bringing different routines, varying boundaries, and multiple authority figures. Thus, the daycare's standards have to be thorough and convincing enough to weather challenges from all. A perfect emblem of my parents' consistency is the single step that separates the family room from the kitchen. The family room is where the kids play, and the kitchen is off-limits except to older children. For thirty years I've watched over four hundred babies test that step, initially as curious crawling but gradually as power struggle with the house rules. As I have witnessed each time, "no" is not something you say once or twice. "No" requires dozens and dozens of repetitions, and the other kids—veterans of the step—must confirm the lesson with each newcomer.

The lesson of that first step led to my own academic discipline. I have achieved a great deal in the classroom—due to talent, due to passion, but primarily due to unwavering consistency. As an undergraduate at Santa Clara University I graduated Summa Cum Laude and was a candidate for valedictorian. I received honors that included induction into Phi Beta Kappa, Alpha Sigma Nu (Jesuit Honors Society), and Sigma Tau Delta (English Honors Society). I had eight poems and an essay of creative non-fiction published in the Santa Clara Review, and I was awarded second prize in UC Berkeley's Ina Coolbrith Poetry Contest. In graduate school at the University of Wisconsin I maintained a 3.86 GPA and achieved a "pass 1" on the comprehensive exam for the master's degree in English literature. I organized conferences and department meetings, and I was elected graduate representative to the university-wide student government council without campaigning, on write-in votes alone. I share these resumé-stuffers because I am extremely proud of my achievements. However, I am prouder of being told by professors that it was a pleasure teaching me; that I made each class visit matter; that I internalized course material and my papers reflected the seriousness with which I treated assignments; that my attentiveness and inquisitiveness were contagious. A professor once told me that great writing was not a product of genius or inspiration as much as it was a product of committed work over the course of many years. I pride myself on my consistency.

Consistency must be matched with purpose, and my parents created the family business with civic responsibility as their guiding light. The families that used our daycare services were in turn employed by the local IBM plant, the Kaiser medical center, construction companies, and city administrations. The parents were mechanics and principals, mid-level managers, and massage therapists. Their children met in our home, a leveling space, and benefited from the mixed experiences of each other. During the summers we enlisted parents to host field trips to their work, so the whole household could spend a special day seeing what they did for a living. Sometimes they brought their work to us, and we would have, for instance, three fire trucks parked in front of the house for a treat. Parents would come bearing the gifts of different cultures, and we might spend a morning learning to make crepes or an afternoon hitting a piñata. Further, my parents forged strong ties with the local public schools, insuring that each kid's teacher was on the same page with her babysitter. Every year we had the grade school's faculty over for a party at the house on the last Friday before Christmas break, an annual event that provides some of my fondest memories of childhood, dissolving the barrier between home and school. We were truly a neighborhood institution. At the "Van Etten Zoo"—as everyone lovingly referred to the daycare—we were not only raising children sixty hours a week; we were also raising good citizens.

I carry this sense of civic responsibility close to heart and it inevitably informs my career endeavors. As two primary examples, I will share my experiences teaching college writing and managing a factory. I spent three years during graduate school at the University of Wisconsin working as a TA with the composition & rhetoric program, teaching the art of written persuasion and introducing eighteen-year-olds to their larger academic community. I created a "globalization" unit for the program, linking the skills of writing with the concerns of world citizenship. I developed a vital classroom community, semester after semester, from which students departed better prepared for leadership in whatever discipline they chose. More recently, I have taken on the task of growing a small factory, focusing on "people AND profits" and developing a competitive manufacturing model that rewards workers fairly. With the owner of BlueFrog Embroidery & Screen-Printing in San Leandro, California, I created a bonus system of employee incentives to boost overall production. I restructured the factory floor to increase efficiency and reduce employee stresses. And most proudly, I developed two employees from unskilled to specialized positions: Laura Vargas worked as garment counter when I arrived a year ago, and now she processes orders on the computer and provides customer service via email; Julio Ramirez worked on the trimming table a year ago and now works as screen-printer's apprentice. Laura always had the owner's trust and merely required skills and literacy training. Julio, by contrast, always had a great work ethic but did not possess the owner's trust—and by extension, the professional behavioral traits that lead to career development. I sat Julio down every several weeks and aggressively coached him with talking points, with the art of question-asking, and with the ethic of enthusiasm to match his work ethic. Julio's gradual rise in the small business is my proudest management success. This sort of success leads to a more thriving and more responsible society.

The home daycare my parents created in my youth guides me to the world I hope to create in the future. In fact, the home daycare is a microcosm of society at large: small businesses are like children, self-interested and individualistic, aspiring to grow and mature; and the rule of law is like a daycare provider, consistent and responsible, nurturing growth and ensuring fair treatment. I enter law school with the dream to someday help provide consistency and fairness to society at large. As a lawyer I will be best equipped to help ensure small businesses have a level playing field and incentives for growth. I believe less in the capital-G "Great Society" than I do in pockets of great society created by all of us with the guidance of a steadily-refined rule of law. If I can achieve for small businesses and those they employ, as a lawyer, even part of what my parents achieved for the children and families they have served these past thirty years, as daycare providers, I will consider my career and my life successful indeed.

David W. (David-son) Van Etten lives near the West Oakland BART station, making it an easy commute to his job at Wells Fargo Bank in downtown San Francisco. He has attended several Compañeros reunions, contributes to companeros-westcoast listserv conversations, and serves as a WCCI director.

The Thing Itself

Nicholas J. Weber

"No, Father! It's the whole thing; the performance itself."

"Then why bother with those parables and the poetry at all?"

A conversation in an adjacent room woke me up. My best friend and business manager, Mitch Kincannon, was entangled in an exchange with our host, the popular and creative chaplain of a South Dakota university where we had played during that very day. Immediately I sensed that the diocesan priest saw his chance to get to the "truth" about this unusual ministry of Nick Weber, SJ, by cornering a lay assistant. What he didn't know was that Mitch had spent years meditating on my own understanding of performance ministry. After all, he'd dedicated—and donated—the most creative years of his life to the Royal Lichtenstein Circus. Eavesdropping on this conversation I discovered that he had made some connections I hadn't.

"The circus performance is a ceremony."

"C'mon! How can you call it that?"

"Look at it. In the middle of the day, in the middle of an over-structured environment, an invitation to play shows up right in the middle of campus."

"So?"

"Well, because the audience is so close to us, and because of the give-and-take banter with the audience, especially Nick's quick repartee, there is a trading off of energies pulling everybody there together. When the skill acts yield the ring to the parables or the poetry, it's really just a shifting of focus, because that energy exchange is still front and center: circus acts or stories are a call to a celebration of imagination and creativity."

Silence. Perhaps the sip of a night-time toddy. Then "I don't see how it relates to God or ministry."

"Play with that imagination thing, Father, and the prominence of creativity in performance art. Creativity. Maybe that's where we're most 'in the image and likeness of . . . '?"

And I fell asleep, only to wake up to thousands of miles of meditation and the years of a few other lifetimes and careers challenged by Mitch's words.

Of course we were messing with ceremony, playing around with ritual. But my over-structured yen for a completely vertical, sequential, hierarchical sense of the sacred had for years embraced only structural elements of faith life. Mine had been a spirituality of connecting dots that didn't relate to me or even to each other. I had missed the dynamite dropped into my younger Jesuit life by the likes of Ignatius Loyola prompting me to "find God in all things!" Gerard Manley Hopkins discovering that the world is "charged" and that "Each mortal being does one thing and the same: /Deals out that being indoors each one dwells." And then Teilhard's fiery "Around the earth, the center of our field of vision, the souls of men form, in some manner, the incandescent surface of matter plunged in God," all got by my day-to-day imagination of my life as spirit.

But I hadn't really missed all that. I knew it. But until I heard Mitch jam the notions of celebration, energy-exchange, play, imagination, and creativity up against one another, I hadn't relaxed enough to enjoy what (who?) was present throughout the tiny circus performances. More importantly, I'd missed out on a much more holistic, peaceful, and affective spirituality. I had tried to eke out priestly self-concepts built on axioms, decrees, models and revelations burdened by centuries of authoritarian interpretations.

Of course it hadn't all been bleak or blind. After all, there was that circus ministry, and it did support some measure of life, light and liveliness for over two decades. But underneath it and beyond it, I had been gifted with a challenge and invitation to get down and divine at a meaningful level with myself and those I loved enough to work for.

And now that I think about it, all that relief, release and recharge came from the brain of a dear friend who could watch a circus more keenly than I, a priest and clown, could.

Nick Weber entered the California Province from Bellarmine College Prep in 1957. He holds an MST from Santa Clara University; MA in drama from San Francisco State University, both in 1970. Ordained in 1970, he founded and toured with Royal Lichtenstein Circus 1971–1993. Nick left the Jesuits in 1993, taught theater arts in Milwaukee from 2001 to 2007, when he retired. In 2012 he published The Circus that Ran Away with a Jesuit Priest: Memoir of a Delible Character. *His latest book is* Shakespeare, with Hearing Aids, Some Old-Timers Revisit the Bard.

A Moment of Truth

Robert J. Willis

I entered the Society directly from high school, a young man in search of a home. Day and night I assiduously sought perfection, the final removal of that last little thing standing between me and Jesus. I would earn an honored place in the long black line here and secure an eternal home hereafter. If trying were enough, I would do enough.

Sheridan, Oregon, novitiate days completed, I began philosophy studies in Spokane. Barely there three months—this was November 1957—I awoke one morning, early. As I lay quietly, I experienced deep down inside me a voice. It made a simple, direct statement: "They're nuts!" It startled me at first. Then a wave of peace flowed through me. My whole being relaxed; I had met the truth.

Over the following months, I mulled over this cryptic message. Who, for example were "they"? I gradually understood them to be the monastic-clerical culture that surrounded me, and its instillers, its proponents, its enforcers. They offered a tempting carrot, belonging; the price: conformity. They also wielded a potent stick: you may have chosen us but we will take our time in choosing you. Beware, unless we approve of you, this home will not be yours. I determined to abandon fear.

What insanity must I reject? From vague ideas at first, I soon found clarity. It reduced to four positions that I must, and would, disavow and change.

I had interpreted detachment, the vow of poverty, the rules of modesty, as requiring impermanence and lack of roots in this earthly life as the necessary means of securing acceptance as a Jesuit and as a

A Moment of Truth

companion of Christ. But Christ, God-with-us, could only be encountered here. I needed to immerse myself in this world in order to meet him. Life must be lived, not passed through.

Remember points and early morning meditation? Proposed as a prayerful encounter with God, in reality, these practices consisted in ruminations about moral positions and explanations. One may conclude with a "colloquy," addressing God directly with a variety of hopes, resolutions, and promises. What I missed, and wanted, was painfully lacking: quiet presence, simple attending to the life in which I "lived and moved and had my being." I would pray, from now on, my way.

As a companion of Jesus, I should love him as my personal savior. If I did so, then I would have no call for developing personal relationships with others, men or women. This would also keep me safe from messy entanglements that could complicate a life of service. But both my heart and my head told me differently. Only by "loving one another as I have loved you," only by being vulnerable to and present to others could I meet Christ. I must set aside safety and certainty; I must embrace the risk of relationship. As a Jesuit priest-psychologist many years later would ask me and himself: "I wonder if it is possible to love God without being in love with another." We both quietly shook our heads: "No."

I had enjoyed four years of carefree living as a Jesuit. I had a place to sleep, decent clothes, passable meals. I didn't have to work to earn a living. I had only one responsibility: do what I'm told. The ones doing the telling reminded us often that obeying them was obeying God: the superior's will is God's will. This troubled me in two ways. As regards God, in the face of clearly absurd commands I could only wonder about the supposed divine perfection; as regards myself, I realized that to give over personal ownership of my choices spelled both irresponsibility and an arrested adolescence. I would, hereafter, listen to superiors and others; I would take in their information and viewpoints, I would then make my own choices as to my own reasonable and conscientious stance. I could not be committed to God, to the Society, or to others unless I was willing to be committed to myself.

I remained in the Society for fifteen more years. I respected Ignatius the visionary, the mystic, and the teacher. I set aside Ignatius the soldier. I didn't want to be a marine either.

Two little words in 1957 changed my life.

Bob Willis entered the Oregon Province in 1953 and departed from it in 1972. That same year he completed his doctoral studies in psychology; he also married Patricia Cannon, a former Religious of the Sacred Heart from Chicago. He and Pat lived on the East Coast during their working years. He taught psychology and religious psychology in a number of colleges, directed a college counseling center, and was executive director of a pastoral counseling center. In addition, he spent a number of years as a psychotherapist in private practice.

The Common Good

William J. Wood, SJ

The following is a series of excerpts from Fr. Wood's 1992 essay *Three Sets of Propositions on Agriculture, the Common Good, and the Task of the Church in Truth-telling and Reconciliation.*

We need to see what we see, hear what we hear, know what we know—and speak the truth: Everything is falling apart, the political system is broken, we're in a mess economically, forty million North Americans (six million Californians) cannot afford basic health care, our institutions are failing us—including the family, the school and university, and religion. There is no vision. There are no leaders. No one seems to know what to do. . . .

One of the most damaging characteristics of the market-system/industrialist mentality is that, boasting of its fairness and objectivity, it denies personal consciousness; using the rhetoric of freedom, it excludes economic necessities from the range of human rights. In the name of separation of church and state, it prevents considerations of spiritual values and social impact from entering into economic decision-making; under the guise of secular autonomy, it has turned the market into an idol. Until the prevailing world-view changes in a revolutionary manner, along with the values that spring from it, there will be no changing of the unjust and unsustainable policies and practices which characterize most of California agriculture.

Some of the most deplorable realities are experienced by landless farm workers. . . . The farm problem is a universal crisis, a critical juncture for Earth and, particularly, for the human species. The urban-rural connection consists in more than the fact that city-folk depend on food production just as much as farmers and others who live in rural areas. Some of the worst problems of the inner cities, here in the US and in Third World countries, can be directly traced to problems in agriculture and the problems of agriculture. At root, the problems in contemporary agriculture are not only structural and systemic, nor merely the symptoms of paradigms that no longer work. They stem, as Wendell Berry raises our sights to see, from a failure of the human spirit....

We are witnessing the demise of political and economic paradigms that have governed human affairs, including agriculture, for centuries. These paradigms are grounded in the technocratic, mechanistic world-view that has prevailed during the second half of this millennium, working on the unquestioned assumptions that the material universe is inanimate and that knowledge itself is reduced to scientific research and description. This is the ideology driving modern industrial society, in which social policy and political debate are based on scientific models of nature and society, divorced from the "seeing" of personal experience and the "knowing" of interpersonal relationships.

Nobody, I think, can fail to see that the central question for Christianity today is to decide what attitude believers will adopt towards this recognition of the value of the Whole, this preoccupation with the Whole.
—Pierre Teilhard de Chardin

What we are facing in the United States and in California today are economic and political structures that, instead of favoring the common good, have been privatized and put at the service of the privileged minorities who appropriate for themselves the material resources of the common good. Therefore, there is no way of arriving at the common good except by overcoming whatever is causing the injustice. In this country, there is the possibility of changing this situation democratically and non-violently, but that will have to happen from local grassroots citizen democracy, from the bottom up, with the leadership of women and people of color, and with dramatic shifts in the way we think and the way we live and work together.

Our prime teacher in the quest for the common good may be the Earth herself, Mother Nature. The environmental crisis is one of those signs of the times that offers an unprecedented *kairos*, a unique moment of opportunity and grace. The very reason that we have lost a sense of citizenship for the common good of human society may be the abdication of our citizenship in the community of creation, which began in the Garden of Eden and gained theological and philosophical respectability five hundred years ago. When we recover our home within the land community (ecology) and as children of the universe (cosmology), we may learn to solve the problems in and of agriculture (technology, economics, and politics).

I've focused my energies on service of the poor and social justice for over forty years. I was first introduced to both practices as a high school student in post-World War II Los Angeles. What I originally conceived of as a special call to "Catholic Action" over and above the basics necessary to save one's soul, evolved for me— as for so many others— in the light of the Second Vatican Council into the very essence of Christian discipleship, "faith doing justice." The struggle to be faithful to this new insight has been twofold. The first, reflected on in some depth by Dietrich Bonhoeffer, has been the temptation to privatize one's religious commitment and keep it out of public life, in this way to keep the powers-that-be off our backs, imagining or pretending that this does not constitute complicity. The second element of the struggle has been to resist both shallow social activism that is not really a proclamation of the Gospel and the more damaging and idolatrous reliance on ideology or fundamentalism instead of on the Gospel. There is something new in the air, however, and it has been gaining on us very rapidly over the past year, stimulated in no small part by reports of global warming and the depletion of the ozone layer. What is new is not the environmental movement, nor the save-the-family-farm movement, nor the promotion of a new paradigm for sustainable agriculture, and certainly not the moral imperative of stewardship. What is new is the growing awareness among believers that God is at work in the agonized groaning of creation, the growing suspicion among non-believers that there is a spiritual, if not religious, dimension to human living, and the growing sense of believers and non-believers alike that everything is connected. What is new in the Church is the dawning of the realization that theology needs to be redone from the bottom up, if it is to be faithful to the living Word that was in the beginning and through Whom all things were made.

Fr. Bill Wood was born and raised in Pennsylvania. His family moved to Pasadena in 1945 and he attended Loyola High School, after which he joined the Jesuits of the California Province in 1951. He was posted at St. Ignatius High School for three years and then returned to Loyola High for two years, before doing his final training at Alma College. He was ordained in 1965 at Blessed Sacrament Church in Hollywood.

From 1969-77 Bill was a Lecturer in Theology and Religious Studies and Director of Campus Ministry at USF. He designed and coordinated an interdisciplinary course on world hunger, involving faculty from various departments. He was a member of the Faculty Senate, developed a master's program in spirituality and was named as an Outstanding Educator of America. He was also the Chaplain at St. Rose Academy and anchored two radio programs on KGO.

Bill left USF to become President and Jesuit Rector at Bellarmine for three years. He founded the Santa Clara Valley Coalition Against Hunger, which over time evolved into the Second Harvest Food Bank (the country's largest). He participated in the 18-month California Food Policy Project, funded by the California Council for the Humanities in Public Policy. The study of solutions to world hunger has been the focus of his career.

From 1984 until 1991 Bill was the Executive Director of the California Catholic Conference of Bishops. He was the advisor to and spokesperson for the 25 bishops of the seven million Catholics living in the 12 dioceses/archdioceses of California regarding public policy issues and relations with the various branches and offices of state government.

During his seven-year term at Santa Clara University he was Director of the University's Eastside Project—now known as The Pedro Arrupe Center for Community-based Learning—and a Bannan Scholar. Then it was back to USF to serve as assistant rector/minister of the Jesuit Community and director of the Mission Council until 2000. Next it was a stint as President at Verbum Dei High School, Los Angeles (Watts). He led a team of Jesuits and lay staff in the conversion of this forty-year-old "Beacon of Hope" in Watts to a jobs-based model. Starting in 2002, he was the tertian instructor for the California Province (Los Gatos, Culver City, Los Angeles), full time, with three tertian groups annually.

A few years ago, Bill was missioned to the Sacred Heart Jesuit Center in Los Gatos, California, where he served as a writer and spiritual director. He died there peacefully on Sunday, June 29, 2014, a few months after his eightieth birthday.

Made in the USA
San Bernardino, CA
03 October 2014